The Performance Consulting Toolbook

The Performance Consulting Toolbook

Carolyn Nilson

McGraw-Hill

New York   San Francisco   Washington, D.C.   Auckland   Bogotá
Caracas   Lisbon   London   Madrid   Mexico City   Milan
Montreal   New Delhi   San Juan   Singapore
Sydney   Tokyo   Toronto

Library of Congress Cataloging-in-Publication Data

Nilson, Carolyn D.
    The performance consulting toolbook / Carolyn Nilson.
        p.   cm.
    Includes bibliographical references and index.
    ISBN 0-07-913760-1.—ISBN 0-07-047169-X (pbk.)
    1. Business consultants.   2. Employees—Training of.   I. Title.
    HD69.C6N55   1999
    658.3´124—dc21   98-44817
                                                                        CIP

McGraw-Hill

A Division of The **McGraw·Hill** Companies

    2 3 4 5 6 7 8 9 0   EDW/EDW   9 0 3 2 1 0 9   (paperback)
1 2 3 4 5 6 7 8 9 0   EDW/EDW   9 0 3 2 1 0 9 8 (looseleaf)

ISBN 0-07-047169-X (paperback)

P/N 047167-3
PART OF
ISBN 0-07-913760-1 (looseleaf)

The sponsoring editor for this book was Richard Narramore, the editing supervisor was Fred Dahl, and the production supervisor was Tina Cameron. It was typeset in New Baskerville by Inkwell Publishing Services.

Printed and bound by Edwards Brothers.

McGraw-Hill Books are available at special quantity discounts to use as premiums and sales promotions, or for use in corporate training programs. For more information, please write to the Director of Special Sales, McGraw-Hill, 11 West 19th Street, New York, NY 10011. Or contact your local bookstore.

To my family:
Lisa,
Kristen, Eric, Jeffrey, Bob,
and Noel—
All high performers who
consistently do good work.

Summary
Contents

Full Contents

Chapter 2:   Human Performance Technology in Plain English   51

Preface: Credit to the Gurus

Men and women who have defined the field of performance consulting/human performance technology for nearly three decades all urge trainers to see a wider horizon. The current excitement in the field of performance consulting is due to dedicated and persistent work by thinkers and doers such as Tom Gilbert, Robert Mager, Joe Harless, Geary Rummler, Gloria Gery, Patricia McLagan, and Dana Gaines Robinson. Others who have greatly influenced the field are my own particular favorites: John Dewey, Benjamin Bloom, J.P. Guilford, Donald Norman, and W. Edwards Deming; also Abraham Maslow, Leonard Nadler, Robert Gagne, Robert Mager, Allison Rossett, Donald Kirkpatrick, Peter Block, Chris Argyris, and Peter Senge. Professional organizations such as the International Society for Performance Improvement (ISPI), the American Society for Training and Development (ASTD), and the Society for Human Resource Management (SHRM) have also played a major role. They have pioneered a broadening of the traditional ideas in training and workplace learning to encompass new visions and new models for human performance, as workers see themselves as owners of a business's most precious resources, as continuous learners, and as initiators of actions that lead to business success and longevity.

This book owes a debt of gratitude to these persons and organizations who have contributed substantially in earlier years to broadening the idea of workplace learning and to those of more recent time who continue to frame the field and lead its practitioners forward. This particular book pays homage to: *John Dewey* (1933), who saw thinking as an active process and attempted to codify the notion of learning to learn; *Benjamin Bloom* (1954), whose taxonomies of educational objectives have endured throughout the growth of training as a profession and have spurred on the idea that learning is made up of many variables of differing suitability; *J. P. Guilford* (1968), who saw intellect in three dimensions, opening the discussion of learning to a multifaceted array of influences; *Thomas Gilbert* (1978), who provided the first model of performance technology; *Robert Mager* (1970, 1973), who focused on how to set objectives and overcome performance gaps in reaching them; *Allison Rossett* (1990), who has tirelessly campaigned for and codified the processes for assessing the needs of learners; and *W. Edwards Deming* (1982), whose quality message for half a century has urged persons at work to break down barriers between organizations, to put everyone to work at improving the company, and to become continuous learners on the job.

This book also acknowledges the specific influence of current thinkers and practitioners: *Peter Block* (1981), whose definition of what makes "flawless consulting" is the standard in the field, particularly for Block's descriptions of the three consultant roles: the "expert," "pair of hands," or "collaborative" (pp. 18ff); *Donald Kirkpatrick* (1994), who has made trainers think beyond the "smiles sheet" for evaluating training's effectiveness; *Donald Norman* (1993), for his leading edge work in cognitive psychology and its manifestations in practical intelligence; *Dana Gaines Robinson* and *James Robinson* (1995), for their efforts in defining "performance consulting" and their tireless promotion of its practices and techniques during the 1990s; and *William Rothwell,* whose prolific work during these last years of the millennium, particularly with the American Society for Training and Development (ASTD), has also advanced the field among professionals who want to change. Assumptions and models on which this book is built have their origins in the work of all of these thinkers and practitioners.

And finally, my great thanks go to my friend, Cindy Burnham-Shaw, a trainer at the top of her field, who is the model for Tina Trainer in Chapter 3.

The Performance Consulting Toolbook

Introduction

From Training Room to Consulting Arena

This book addresses the need for trainers to reorient their thinking from the comfort and structure of the training classroom to the more ambiguous (and exciting!) consulting arena. The gap is actually not nearly as wide as you might think. Trainers have considerable expertise as job and task analysts, learning specialists, facilitators, communication experts, and persons with a broad view of the human dimensions of organizations that generally comes into play during training sessions. Because of their interest, aptitude, and experience, trainers seem naturally to go into performance consulting. Moreover, the training industry is undergoing a shift from an exclusive focus on training as the solution to all or most employee performance problems, to looking for other, cheaper, more effective alternatives to training, such as job aids, work redesign, incentive structures, etc. Whether they want to or not, many trainers are being asked to do less training and more "performance consulting," in which training may be just one of many possible solutions to an employee performance problem.

However, trainers need to know about many cautions and many options before jumping into the new consulting role or making an official career change. This toolbook takes you through the changes you'll need to make to successfully move from training to performance consulting. Various consulting models are discussed, particularly those elaborated by Peter Block (1981, pp. 18ff):

- The extra pair of hands model.

- The favored collaborative model of working either as an insider or outsider.

- The model of the expert from outside the organization or company.

Tools in this volume are at varying levels of sophistication; the book has appeal to newcomers to the field as well as to those who are already functioning as performance consultants.

What Can This Book Do for You?

If you've leafed through this book, you've seen that it's a different kind of book—a *toolbook*. It is crafted especially for the trainer with more than a little curiosity about how to be a good consultant, for the trainer who has some experience and lots of ideas but who just needs a little encouragement and pointing in the right direction. It's a book that can lead you from training straight into performance consulting.

Skimming the book shows you also that full-size worksheets, forms, lists of guidelines, graphic models—a host of knowledge- and skill-building tools—are included, ready to use. No publication on the market today offers such an array of ready-to-run-with consulting tools. The book was designed with great care and understanding of the trainer in career transition. It's a book that's meant to be *used*, not just read. In Part II, a "What You Already Know That Can Help You" section is associated with each tool found there. Throughout, the book takes you from where you are as a training professional and leads you forward into performance consulting, recognizing training's strengths as well as performance consulting's challenges. It contains hundreds of tips for success as a performance consultant; most of all, it gives you accessible, credible, tested, useful tools you can choose to fit your situation.

The book was written as a teaching book. Trainers in career transition tend to be motivated learners. Chapters 1 and 2 define, describe, illustrate, and give examples of two new concepts: consulting and human performance technology. Chapter 3 shows you the application of the merging of consulting and human performance, as "Tina Trainer" takes you through the transition thinking from training to performance consulting. Throughout all these chapters, useful and immediately usable tools are provided to help you clarify your thinking, understand the finer points of new ideas and concepts, and develop new skills. Tina is a bright, experienced trainer with good training instincts. She'll definitely be your buddy as you too go through some of the things she's experienced.

Chapter 4 is devoted to the contracting process, the starting place for serious consulting and perhaps the most unfamiliar area for the trainer. This chapter stands at mid point in the book, and is built on your comprehension and ability to apply what you've learned in Chapters 1, 2, and 3. The "hard core" performance consulting process follows in Chapters 5, 6, and 7, which take you from analysis tasks to the design of solutions, as well as to the associated evaluation and management tasks.

When you've finished with *The Performance Consulting Toolbook*, you will have been an active learner.

Four particular information resources within the book have been designed with special attention for logical readers who like things listed and spelled out:

- An *annotated table of contents*, listing and describing all tools, located in the front of the book.

- A 71-item *Human Performance Glossary* at the end of Chapter 2.

- A *bibliography* of all books referenced in the *Toolbook* and of other books that should be in your performance consulting library, and

- An extensive and comprehensive *index*, generated by the author, recognizing the best of training influences as well as the best of performance consulting.

These reference features of this book can help you stay organized as you move forward through it.

Now Let's Talk about Mind-Bending

Next to the training room, the consulting arena can seem like a lions' den or snake pit. In the familiar training room, the leader (i.e., trainer) is in charge and is well prepared to facilitate an organized delivery of training. This setting is often in sharp contrast to the consulting arena, where leaders (i.e., consultants) more often than not have to negotiate dangers and earn the right to the kind of leadership role they expect to play. Trainees come prepared to accept the authority of the trainer; clients accept their own authority. Trainees generally do what the trainer wants; consultants do what clients want. The two situations do not equate: Trainees don't equal clients.

Trainers who want to become consultants first have to let go of the crutch of lesson plans, trainer's manuals, overheads, lecterns, and other items that give the trainer control. Consultants lead in a different way: They negotiate through a give-and-take dialogue with clients and by being totally sensitive to clients' fears, insecurities, embarrassments, irritabilities, resentments, and the fuzzy logic that often goes along with such emotions. It's fair to say that training is built on a cognitive foundation; consulting generally begins on an emotional foundation. Consultants have to find their way through the clients' complex environment to figure out what the problem is and who can help to solve it. Consultants must be comfortable operating within this "creative mess" of personal and organizational influences, unlike trainers who generally operate in a very structured and planned environment.

So how do you, as the trainer eager to flex a little muscle and give performance consulting a try, begin to prepare yourself? First, you need to understand that, as a consultant, you have to deal with both the ambiguities of the client environment and the ultimate need to be a focused and clear thinker about choosing interventions that can improve performance. That is, you must be both a divergent thinker and a convergent thinker. These are skills that you can develop and practice. Trainers turned consultants often lack experience with divergent thinking. The tools in Chapter 1 show you the differences and help you to prepare mentally for consulting's challenges. Chapter 3 also helps with this.

Another critical difference between training and consulting is how time is used and valued. Think about how you plan your training program or course, especially one that extends over a day or several days. You probably think in terms of 1-hour segments, interspersed with coffee breaks and lunch. You collect your trainer's salary at the end of the pay period, irrespective of what happened or didn't happen during those time segments. Trainers generally are not held accountable for what was or wasn't learned by trainees. On the other hand, a consultant is held accountable for what happens during consulting time. A performance consulting contract based on a per-diem or per-hour fee obligates you to produce value for each hour charged. That's a very different way of thinking about time, and often trainers-turned-consultants have to "tighten up" their concept of time to be successful. Consultants don't get paid unless they deliver value. The tools in Chapters 1 and 4 help you with issues of time.

Trainers spend a lot of energy, time, and resources investigating and codifying learning. Performance consultants deal with performance. "Performance" is a broader term. Learning sometimes has a relationship to performance, but sometimes it doesn't. Trainers who become successful performance consultants have to give up their bias toward learning. They must realize that performance problems might be caused by any number of variables, including bad equipment, overwork, lack of appreciation, cumbersome procedures, inappropriate placement in a job, poor lighting, and so on.

The tools in Chapter 2 help you see clearly what performance means. This chapter, "Human Performance Technology in Plain English," deals with all the important terms and concepts of the field. The goal of Chapter 2 is to lay out the definers and describers of the field, to present the knowledge base of human performance technology, and to illustrate its multifaceted nature through checklists, guidelines, and various graphics. Chapter 2 is meant to draw a big luminous circle around the field and include many points of light within it. When you finish with Chapter 2, you should have a pretty good idea of what the field of human performance is all about, and begin to see clearly that it differs from training. You can refer to the glossary at the end of this chapter, as you later follow the steps toward performance consulting.

Finally, the specialized skills of performance consulting are different from the skills of designing and delivering training. Trainers have a narrow focus on the training program or course itself; performance consultants must have a wide angle that encompasses the client's business goals and past performance vis á vis competitors. Consultants have to see the big picture. Trainers think in terms of objectives for the learners; performance consultants think in terms of operational processes and even of the political and economic change drivers that influence how groups or individuals at work perform. Trainers think in terms of a lesson unfolding or of clever ways to elaborate content; consultants think in terms of problem identification and solution finding. The tools in Chapters 5, 6, and 7 help you develop the specialized skills of performance consulting.

This Book Is about Doing

Above all, this book is about *doing*. That's what "performance" means. Think about it: Persons at work are fundamentally engaged in *doing* their jobs, not in just *being* at work. Human resources specialists, trainers, supervisors, and all others in leadership positions regarding how people do their jobs must also think like doers. It is especially critical for you, the trainer who wants to become a performance consultant, to refocus your thinking before trying to do the work of a consultant. This book leads you gently through this transition in perspective, giving you tools in a systematic way that help you see exactly what kinds of things you need to do.

The role of performance consultant—one who facilitates *doing* better work—is a role that can be adopted by anyone with any job title. All that it requires is an action mindset, a clear understanding of the many factors in workplace performance, and a good set of facilitation tools. This book offers the set of tools—tools you can use.

Catching and Riding the Performance Wave

The Performance Consulting Toolbook came into being because the jargon of the field is coming close to interfering with widespread progress. We need to be doing more and posturing less. There's a need for an explanation of how to do performance consulting, with associated tools that can be easily adapted to many business situations by persons with many job titles as well as by those who just want the title of "consultant."

There's a need for practical tools presented in a way that makes their use seem easy, logical, full of common sense—tools that make the action and risk taking of consulting exactly the kinds of workplace behavior that you want for yourself. This toolbook fills that need. This book is especially designed for trainers who want to become performance consultants. It is expressly meant for you, who want to change and go with the action.

If you'd like to see if this book's for you, check out the following sample of the kinds of tools you'll find here. They illustrate the diversity of approaches to performance consulting skill building that you'll find among the rest of the tools in this book.

- *Tool 3.7   Final Words of Support for New Performance Consultants:* This tool comes at the end of a chapter that focuses on ways in which a trainer changes her thinking to become a performance consultant. This tool is a *summarizing tool,* one that succinctly states key strategies for thinking and acting as you approach a performance consulting job. This tool, like other summarizing tools in the book, offers *friendly advice* as well as plenty of the *you-can-do-it attitude!*

- *Tool 4.4   Kinds of Data to Avoid in Contracting:* This type of tool is a *simple checklist.* There are many tools of this format in the *Toolbook.* This one has the added interest of being written from the point of view of what to avoid. Often it's easier to see "the right" from having first seen "the wrong." Checklists of all sorts are found throughout the book, encouraging the reader's active learning and decision making as you use each checklist.

- *Tool 4.8   How to Organize and Use Data for Contracting:* This tool gives you specific 1-2-3 *steps to follow* as you carry out a plan for organizing data you've collected.

- *Tool 6.15   Scales and Rating Systems:* This tool is a set of four *graphic representations* of scales and rating systems that are useful in measurement and in reporting of diagnostic activities. Numerous graphics are included as tools in this book—we've made a conscious effort to appeal to those readers who like to learn this way.

- *Tool 6.19   Source of Causes Chart:* This chart is typical of other *documentation forms* found throughout the *Toolbook.* This tool, however, has the added dimension of *assessment,* requiring the user to rate documented items on an "importance scale." Other documentation forms also require interactive judgment on the part of the performance consultant—tools like this one are designed to move you forward into the next step of performance consulting.

- *Tool 7.4   Improvement Proposal:* This kind of tool can best be characterized as *insider savvy.* This particular tool gives you the good words to use in your improvement proposal, and tells you how to structure the proposal. Tools like this type of tool synthesize the field's best practices for you and show you how to make the best use of what we've all learned to date about performance consulting.

The Growth of Performance Consulting

At the highest levels of corporations and agencies, there is much discussion today about the value of human resources, elevating them in business parlance to the level of capital resources and financial resources. The "knowledge economy" and "intellectual capital" are terms with more teeth these days than ever before. Chief knowledge officers enjoy visibility, respect, pay, and high position in more and more companies. Strategic measures are being taken throughout leading companies in corporate America to identify, develop, maintain, and protect a company's strategic knowledge advantage. Corporate planners and human resource leaders are collaborating in new ways to preserve and continuously encourage the creation of deeper, broader, higher-quality, and more bottom-line-useful intellectual capital. It is a very good time for analysts, designers, and service providers who can figure out how human performance directly affects business performance. It is a time for action, for paying more attention to how people do their jobs and why they do them well or poorly—for performance consulting.

At the front lines of action in corporations and agencies, employees are challenged as never before to perform—to do more work better. Employees are expected to know how the business works, not just to know how to do the tasks of their jobs. For many, it is a confusing time when the social contracts, agreements, and expectations of employer–employee relationships are uncomfortably changing and becoming murky. It's a time for people who can seize the moment and clarify issues, in the name of improving organizational and individual performance.

In many companies, people need help in focusing on exactly how to do better work. Corporate leaders often need to know what supports to put in place for front-line workers to function as business people, not just as masters of the tasks that make up their jobs. Executives, managers, and employees are investing more energy, thought, and resources in developing human performance. It is a time for action, for vision, for creativity, and for collaboration.

Integrating New Ideas and Acting Now

In such changing times, the business's corporate culture becomes vitally important to human performance. What happens around the people in a company affects how they perform the tasks and processes of their work. Numerous business writers over the past decade have called analysis of corporate culture by various names, and have elaborated specific parts of it in an effort to describe and explain how organizations work. Some terms from the broader professional literature that are now part of the performance consulting dialogue are "systems thinking," "learning organization," "organization development," "change management," "intervention," "synergy," "partnering."

Downsizing and outsourcing put enormous pressures on human resources and organization development specialists to facilitate peak performance from vendors as well as from employees. Trainers, particularly trainers with instructional design and development expertise, are uniquely poised in an organization to lead performance improvement efforts. But trainers must think differently, and above all *act* differently, to do consulting work.

Part I
Moving from Training to Performance Consulting

Three chapters make up Part I. The first two deal with the twin concepts of "consultant" and "performance."

Chapter 1, "Turning a Trainer into a Consultant," provides 16 tools to help you make the transition from trainer to consultant.

Chapter 2, "Human Performance Technology in Plain English," defines, explains, and elaborates on the meaning of performance in human resource terms. This chapter also synthesizes ideas in professional practice, providing the context and tools for realizing the dimensions of human performance as a technology—human performance technology. This chapter provides 15 tools and a "Human Performance Glossary."

Chapter 3, "Tina Trainer Tries the Tools," is a plausible set of scenarios showing how a trainer thinks and acts as she becomes a performance consultant, using some of the 34 performance consulting tools in Chapters 1 and 2. Chapter 3 concludes with "Final Words of Support for New Performance Consultants." Taken together, these three chapters form the fundamentals of understanding and action for getting into performance consulting.

Chapter 1

Turning a Trainer into a Consultant

In this chapter you'll find forms, checklists, worksheets, and job aids to help you think like a performance consultant and move forward with this thinking into performing any one of the various roles a consultant must perform. By design, this chapter talks a lot about training and what you need to do as you transition yourself into a new role. It also quickly moves within each tool from the perspective of training to that of performance consulting. Each tool included here is presented with a "left-hand page" giving an overview of its purpose, why the tool is important, and an example or sample of how to use it in a typical performing consulting situation. A "right-hand page" provides the tool itself in an immediately usable form for easy removal and copying for use in your own organization or for your own personal use.

Tools in Chapter 1

1.1 Self-Assessment Checklist on Trainers, Trainees, Consultants, Clients

Description

This checklist helps you see the differences among these four types of roles, particularly between trainer and consultant and between trainee and client.

Why This Tool Is Important

This tool helps you reaffirm where you stand as a trainer and see where you need to go as a consultant. It is a template for easing you through a change in thinking from trainer and trainee to consultant and client.

Example of How to Use This Tool

This is meant to be a self-assessment tool, for you to reflect on your understanding of your job roles point by point. Before you check off any item, take time to reflect on its meaning and to what extent you think it is true and applies to you. Follow up on any item that you question, gathering input from colleagues or from additional reading so that you fully comprehend the meaning of that item before you go on to the next.

For example, you might find that you're not sure about item 3 under "Trainers":

___   **3.** A trainer's main focus is teaching.

You find that you have acted more often as a facilitator of group dynamics than as a teacher. You question whether your own main focus has been teaching. You need to talk with some other trainers to see how they view the main focus of the trainer—generically as well as in their own specific jobs. You're willing to accept item number 3, but you just need professional input. You find that one of your trainer friends discovered in talking with you about this tool that he never functioned as a teacher; his job was to review the contracts of vendors from the outside who periodically provided training services to your company. He functioned as an administrator, certainly not as a teacher. You're even willing to accept that maybe you haven't been doing the job of a trainer—that maybe you've actually been doing something else, although your title, like your friend's, is "trainer."

To use this tool effectively, you need to go through a careful self-assessment on each item in the checklist. Self-awareness is a critical starting place for honest consulting.

Self-Assessment Checklist on Trainers, Trainees, Consultants, Clients

Instructions: Use this checklist as a self-assessment tool to demonstrate your present perspective on the differences between training and consulting. It may be helpful to view the checklist as two sets of checklists, one focusing primarily on trainers and the other on consultants. As you go through the lists, note any items that make you hesitate. Be sure that you clarify in your own mind the differences suggested by any questionable item before you continue checking yourself. Place a checkmark next to each item when you are satisfied that you understand what it means.

Trainers
___ 1. A trainer is a teacher.
___ 2. A trainer absorbs a specific body of information to be taught.
___ 3. A trainer's main focus is teaching.
___ 4. A trainer masters presentation skills for maximum effectiveness.
___ 5. A trainer facilitates various kinds of learning: computer-based, on-the-job, one-to-one, small group, large group, distance learning, learning at conferences.
___ 6. A trainer seeks evaluation feedback on her/his presentation skills and content expertise and uses it in future instructional design.
___ 7. A trainer's focus is primarily narrow—on content that has been identified as someone's need to know.

Trainees
___ 1. A trainee is a learner.
___ 2. The trainee is primarily concerned with the acquisition of new knowledge, new skills, and sometimes new attitudes.
___ 3. Trainees exhibit various learning styles that affect how they learn.
___ 4. A trainee engages in training to improve performance in his/her present job.
___ 5. A trainee also engages in development activities to further her/his long-range career opportunities.

Consultants
___ 1. A consultant is a salesperson.
___ 2. A consultant's antennae reach throughout an organization.
___ 3. A consultant has a client and sometimes more than one client.
___ 4. A consultant's roles vary. They typically include being an extra pair of hands, being an action-oriented collaborator with a client, and being an expert outsider.
___ 5. A consultant's job is to advise, to support, to intervene, and to leverage.
___ 6. A consultant is not part of an organization.
___ 7. A consultant has influence, not control.
___ 8. A consultant provides contractual services and products and is evaluated on their quality and timeliness.

Clients
___ 1. A client is a buyer, a shopper, a consumer.
___ 2. A client is an accountable member of an organization.
___ 3. A client is primarily concerned with value.
___ 4. A client is also concerned with a consultant's output and effect.
___ 5. A client is the keeper of corporate intellectual property, and of physical and financial resources.
___ 6. A client calls the shots.

1.2 Chart of Differences between Presentation/Training Skills and Troubleshooting/Consulting Skills

Description

This chart is a reminder of key differences between a trainer's presentation skills set and a performance consultant's troubleshooting skills set.

Why This Tool Is Important

Trainers need presentation skills; consultants need troubleshooting skills. Trainers who are new to performance consulting often tend to revert to trainer behavior and confuse the trainer's skill set with the skill set required of a consultant. For trainers to effectively move away from reliance on a familiar training skill set and to reliance on a new consulting skill set, they need to know the characteristics of each. Both trainer and consultant must deal with essentially three variables: relationships, content, and support materials. This chart is meant to simply point out the obvious differences in skills required to deal effectively with these variables; it is also designed to be a quick reminder of a trainer's need to refocus prior to engaging as a consultant. Think of this as a job aid for yourself listing the skills you'll need and how they differ from those that you currently have. But don't be discouraged. There is a lot of overlap between the two skill sets!

Examples of How to Use This Tool

Suppose you were asked to find out why a particular group of customer service representatives in your company get an unusually high number of complaints from customers about the service they provide over the telephone when the customer service hotline is called.

A *trainer's approach* might be to imagine how the proper skills of customer service could be taught to this group of employees. A trainer would assume (or might have been told by the employees' manager) that the employees were performing poorly because they didn't know what they should be doing. A trainer would think in terms of presentation. A trainer would begin to think about how to design a course or perhaps a video feedback exercise to help the employees learn the proper skills to do their job. A trainer focuses on skills and knowledge.

A *consultant's approach* might begin with setting up a time to observe the employees doing their work. Then he/she might determine how long these persons have been employed, when and by whom they were originally trained to do their job, whether their procedures book reflected current policies, where these employees stood on the salary scale, whether they were shift workers and if this was by their choice, how often and by whom they received performance reviews, and who their supervisors have been since they joined the company. A consultant surveys the big picture, and makes no assumptions about training. A consultant focuses on analyzing the overall work environment.

Chart of Differences between Presentation/Training Skills and Troubleshooting/Consulting Skills

Instructions: Use this chart as a matrix exercise to review the main characteristics of each kind of skill set. Refer to it prior to each occasion in which you are functioning as a consultant.

Differences between Presentation Skills and Troubleshooting Skills		
	Presentation Skills	*Troubleshooting Skills*
Relationships	• Manage group dynamics • Motivate individuals to learn. • Pace and focus lessons. • Vary teaching style to accommodate learning style. • Seek and use feedback from learners.	• Analyze group dynamics. • Question individuals for relevant information, build networks. • Look at the big picture of business relationships. • Generate options for acceptance by clients. • Seek and use feedback from clients.
Content	• Teach to learning objectives. • Follow course outline. • Differentiate cognitive, psychomotor, and value-based skills, and teach each appropriately.	• Determine project parameters. • Define problems. • Collect, sort, and evaluate data.
Support materials	• Review media that support the course for graphic layout, clarity of ideas, gender bias, timeliness. • Practice using media and machines. • Use media to engage learners and support learning.	• Identify and find key data and personal sources. • Verify sources. • Use material to develop plans.

1.3 Worksheet on Thinking Styles: Convergent versus Divergent Thinking

Description

This worksheet helps you determine whether your thinking style is more like that of a trainer (convergent) or a consultant (divergent).

Why This Tool Is Important

To understand your thinking style, begin with understanding the basics of convergent thinking and of divergent thinking. Essentially these terms from cognitive science mean what they imply: convergent thinking converges on a point, and divergent thinking diverges from a point. The concepts of convergence and divergence are found in many aspects of life, and generally illustrate opposing ways of going about things.

In the transition from trainer to consultant, these two ways of thinking are important to recognize in yourself and in others. A great deal of professional literature in the field of learning theory and practice has developed over the years on these concepts. One example is the experimental work done in brain hemispheric lateralization, known in popular terms as the debate over left brain–right brain capabilities; the left brain is generally more related to convergent thinking and the right brain is generally more related to divergent thinking. Another is the body of educational psychology that is popularized in the ideas and practices of action-reflection learning, where action is more convergence and reflection is more divergence. Another is psychological type, following Jung, Myers, and Briggs.

Trainers most often have a convergent thinking orientation; consultants most often have a divergent thinking orientation. For example, trainers expect a "best" or "correct" answer to a question or solution to a problem; they follow a plan to a logical conclusion. Consultants tend to generate options and estimate their plausibility; they evaluate, prioritize, and synthesize. Trainers follow a prescribed process and content outline; consultants create their own timelines based on the dimensions of the project. Consultants eventually must be intellectually facile in operating as both convergent and divergent thinkers, but they must begin with a mindset of divergence. This tool helps you sort out the differences and determine where you are personally.

Example of How to Use This Tool

After your self-assessment, a self-development plan might contain items like this:

Plans for developing divergent thinking:			
What?	*When?*	*With Whom?*	*Why?*
Go to meeting without notes	Tuesday	Phil, Richard, Mary	To see if I can take the broader view

Worksheet on Thinking Styles: Convergent versus Divergent Thinking

Instructions: Use this worksheet to rate your natural tendency to think in a particular way. Simply place a mark on the line after each statement indicating your self-rating of the item. Use a 4-point scale, where 1 = never and 4 = always; a mark anywhere on the line is acceptable. There are no right or wrong responses; use the results of your work to make plans to develop your capacity for divergent thinking if your patterns are overwhelmingly convergent. This worksheet is appropriate for use in team training.

	1 = Never	2 = Sometimes	3 = Often	4 = Always

Convergent Thinking

1. I like to follow directions.
2. I feel best when "loops" are closed.
3. I plan carefully to finish lessons.
4. I prefer concrete to abstract.
5. I like to take things to logical conclusions.
6. I need everything in order before I begin.

Divergent Thinking

7. I work best from my own intuition.
8. I thrive on variety.
9. I like to generate options.
10. I prefer synthesis over analysis.
11. "Big pictures" fascinate me.
12. Freedom is more important to me than discipline.

Plans for developing divergent thinking:

What?	When?	With Whom?	Why?

-
-
-
-
-

1.4 Would You Hire You? Conditions and Roles for *Internal* Consulting

Description

This chart is useful for a trainer/consultant who needs to "walk in the manager's shoes." It is written from the perspective of the manager who is considering hiring consulting services and asks, "What are the qualities of the right person for the job?"

Why This Tool Is Important

This tool is included early in the chapter to help you get into the skin of a client. Often trainers make the transition to performance consultant by becoming internal consultants. A current trend is for entire training departments to become an internal performance consulting group. Before a manager makes this structural move, a good deal of questioning takes place about the conditions that may or may not be present for effective consulting. This tool gives you a chance to play the role of a manager who is considering you for the position of internal performance consultant.

Example of How to Use This Tool

Scenario: Upon reviewing Chart 1.4, you, the manager and a potential internal consulting client, realize that you have serious questions about conditions number 1 and 6. You realize that the staff person you are considering is a stellar performer as an instructor in the management development curriculum, but has had very little experience in ten years in the company in any organization other than training. By sheer force of personality and reputation, this person seems the logical choice to be the company's first performance consultant. From where you stand, however, you are unsure whether this person has the other competencies and skills for successful consulting. Your experience with consultants from the outside is that they get battered around pretty badly at this company, and you're not sure whether this internal person can stand the fence-sitting, vacillation, and blame that generally go along with consultant work. Maybe you should investigate further—maybe go with an external consultant again. Maybe you have to look more deeply into this person's broader competency as a consultant.

You have legitimate and understandable concerns about conditions 1 and 6:

XX? **1.** Present staff has the competencies and skills to handle the job.

XX? **6.** Present staff is not constrained by its present position or reputation.

Would You Hire You?
Chart of Conditions and Roles for *Internal* Consulting

Instructions: Refer to this chart and to Tool 1.5 on page 20, before you decide to engage any consultant, internal or external. Let these two charts be your decision-making aid.

Internal Consulting

Conditions

1. Present staff has the competencies and skills to handle the job.
2. Present staff has a wide network of colleagues.
3. Present staff is able to cross levels for information and service.
4. Present staff is trustworthy and engenders trust.
5. Present staff has its management's unconditional support (time, pay, project budget, ability to travel, resources, freedom of choice).
6. Present staff is not constrained by its present position or reputation.
7. Present staff wants to do the job.

Roles

8. Needs analyst.	16. Extra pair of hands and feet.
9. Negotiator.	17. Project designer.
10. Diplomat.	18. Project manager.
11. Interviewer.	19. Communication channel.
12. Feedback specialist.	20. Collaborator with other leaders.
13. Facilitator.	21. Subject matter expert.
14. Interpreter.	22. Change agent.
15. Evaluator.	

1.5 Would You Hire You? Conditions and Roles for *External* Consulting

Description

This chart is useful for a consultant who needs to "walk in the manager's shoes." It is written from the perspective of the manager who is considering contracting for consultant services. It lists the basic considerations forming the background for whether to look outside the company for help.

Why This Tool Is Important

Like Tool 1.4 on internal consulting, this tool can be used by the trainer who needs to understand what a potential consulting client considers when hiring an external consultant. It shows how a manager might think before contacting you, the performance consultant. Taken together, these two tools can help you, the trainer, decide which kind of consulting—internal or external—might be better for you.

Example of How to Use This Tool

Scenario: Your potential client, the manager, takes a look at her organization, does a quick assessment of the morale around the office, and concludes that only an outsider could hope to fix some of the problems she sees. She zeroes in on four of the roles listed in Tool 1.5:

  8. Needs analyst.

  10. Diplomat.

  14. Interpreter.

  18. Advocate; cheerleader.

This might have been her thought process:

> **Number 18, Advocate; cheerleader.** *That's what we need! We don't need an expert or even a super facilitator type. What we need is simply an outsider who can help us see what we do around here that is right. Morale has been so bad—we need that fixed too—but what we really need is someone who can act as an advocate for our good work and be a cheerleader throughout the organization. The present employees need a lift; current staff will have no credibility in performing this function. An outsider is the only choice. Now ... if we can find just the right person who is also a good* needs analyst *[number 8],* interpreter *[number 14], and* diplomat *[number 10], we'll be all set.*

Your task, then, in deciding whether you want to be considered for such a set of roles, is to examine your own competencies, especially those of needs analysis and diplomacy. Trainers generally do not get involved very much with either of these, and you might have to get additional training yourself in these two areas. If you've been a successful classroom trainer, you probably have good skills as an interpreter of information and as a cheerleader. Honest self-appraisal is critical. This tool can help.

Would You Hire You?
Conditions and Roles for *External* Consulting

Instructions: Refer to this chart and to Tool 1.4 on page 18 before you decide to engage any consultant, internal or external. Let these two charts be your decision-making aid.

Conditions
1. Present staff does not have the competencies and skills to handle the job.
2. An outsider has a better chance of establishing rapport with key people.
3. Company culture is open enough to allow access to an outsider.
4. The outsider's reputation and references as a consultant are of high quality.
5. Top management is committed to using external consultants and has whatever resources might be necessary.
6. Present staff is accustomed to working with outsiders.
7. Present staff does not want to do the job.

Roles

8. Needs analyst.	16. Extra pair of hands and feet.
9. Negotiator.	17. Project designer.
10. Diplomat.	18. Advocate; cheerleader.
11. Interviewer.	19. Salesperson.
12. Feedback specialist.	20. Collaborator with staff.
13. Facilitator.	21. Subject matter expert.
14. Interpreter.	22. Change agent.
15. Evaluator.	

1.6 "Pair of Hands" Consulting Checklist

Description

This checklist helps you to know what to expect if you accept a consulting assignment just to get a foot in the door. It characterizes the "pair of hands" consultant who generally works under close supervision in a narrow project.

Why This Tool Is Important

While an extra pair of hands is not what you generally think of as consulting (most people like to see themselves as the outside expert), the model is used quite often. It is important to the new consultant because that extra pair of hands is often a way to gain entry into a company. If you do a good job in a supervised, very specific, and often narrow assignment, you might have a shot at a broader consulting job later. Some examples are writing the corporate annual report, debugging an order-entry system, creating documentation and user manuals for the new personnel data system, administering the Myers-Briggs type inventory to all supervisors, tabulating an employee opinion survey and preparing an executive summary of it.

Example of How to Use This Tool

As you review this checklist, three items jump out as things you can't stand:

____ **1.** The client is always close at hand.

____ **3.** The consultant responds to the initiative of the client.

____ **6.** The consultant has limited visibility in the company.

Your reflection on the "pair of hands" consulting model might go like this:

Upon review, items 1, 3, and 6 jump out as the defining characteristics of a potential engagement with this company as a "pair of hands" consultant. When I look at these three in isolation from the other items in the checklist, I realize that this is not what I want or expect from a consulting contract. I believe that I am not cut out to be a "pair of hands" consultant because I see myself as more creative than this role allows, and I am looking for wider and deeper access in the company. I do not think that this kind of consulting, even though it is a foot in the door, will do me or this company any good in the long run.

"Pair of Hands" Consulting Checklist

Instructions: Review this checklist prior to either contracting for this kind of consultant or being this kind of consultant. Place a checkmark next to each item in the checklist that you are prepared to accept. There are constraints and limitations to this kind of consulting; go into it with eyes open.

❑ 1. The client is always close at hand.

❑ 2. The client determines the agenda, the goal, the process, the plan.

❑ 3. The consultant responds to the initiative of the client.

❑ 4. The consultant has little creative flexibility.

❑ 5. The consultant makes few decisions about organizational change.

❑ 6. The consultant has limited visibility in the company.

❑ 7. The consultant's contract is narrow in scope.

❑ 8. The consultant takes what the client gives in terms of assumptions about causes, effects, evaluation, and future action.

❑ 9. The consultant primarily works *for* the client, not *with* the client.

1.7 Collaborative Consulting Checklist

Description

This checklist contains items that show that the consultant is in a 50/50 relationship with the client. It characterizes the "collaborative" consultant, the preferred model for performance consulting.

Why This Tool Is Important

The consultant as collaborator is the preferred model for performance consulting. Trainers typically understand this at an intellectual level, but seldom at an emotional level. Trainers are used to being in-charge leaders of the training situation, and they are often loners when it comes to being part of a corporate network of influence. Trainers also often get impatient with situations that are not well-designed, which they will find in most of the early stages of performance consulting in the collaborative model. Flexibility is often the key to success; the trainers' discipline of carefully constructed learning opportunities, courses, and programs has not been a training ground for flexibility. Trainers who become collaborative performance consultants need to constantly check themselves to be sure that they are in a 50/50 relationship with their clients.

Example of How to Use This Tool

As you review this checklist, two items cause you some concern. These are:

2. Client and consultant are prepared to invest the extra time that collaboration requires.

3. Collaboration means shared responsibility and accountability for analysis, planning, implementation, and evaluation of results.

Your reflection upon this collaborative consulting model might go like this:

Items 2 and 3 are of major concern prior to entering a collaborative consulting contract. I'm not sure how to write the contract so that the time is flexible. This will have to be controlled perhaps by the discipline of project reports/meetings at least every two weeks. Likewise, with joint accountability: standards, expectations, and accountability procedures will have to be agreed on and strictly followed.

Collaborative Consulting Checklist

Instructions: Review this checklist prior to either contracting for this kind of consultant or being this kind of consultant. Place a checkmark next to each item in the checklist that you are prepared to accept. Performance consulting generally is this kind of consulting; before entering into collaborative consulting, be sure that you can and want to be this kind of consultant.

- ❏ 1. Client and consultant agree that collaboration is essential to success.
- ❏ 2. Client and consultant are prepared to invest the extra time that collaboration requires.
- ❏ 3. Collaboration means shared responsibility and accountability for analysis, planning, implementation, and evaluation of results.
- ❏ 4. Control is shared by client and consultant.
- ❏ 5. Client and consultant can both expect to become learners during collaborative consulting; this differs from the consultant as teacher.
- ❏ 6. Resources (time, dollars, personnel) are allocated by the joint decision of client and consultant.
- ❏ 7. Information requests are issued jointly by client and consultant.
- ❏ 8. Communication is planned and implemented jointly by client and consultant.
- ❏ 9. Both client and consultant carefully attend the processes of collaboration.

1.8 Consulting Checklist for Experts

Description

This checklist helps you to see the pitfalls of the expert model of consulting, a model often assumed by clients and sometimes required in performance consulting.

Why This Tool Is Important

Those who are just beginning to think about being a consultant most often think of being this kind of consultant: the expert, usually from the outside. When you examine the expert role, however, you see that this kind of consulting has traps and that it often doesn't turn out to be the wonderfully fulfilling role you'd imagined. One of the main pitfalls of this model is that the consultant often becomes a scapegoat. Staff can easily develop the attitude "if you know so much about it, why haven't you fixed it?" Sometimes a different consulting model, such as the collaborator, might enable the consultant to take the time to work with the staff to uncover all the performance problems and their causes and to jointly work on fixing the problems.

Example of How to Use This Tool

As you review this checklist, you react favorably to most of the items, but numbers 4 and 5 stick out as potentially troublesome:

4. Who the client is often becomes a mystery.

5. Posturing and politicking by staff often occur.

Your reflection upon this expert model might include such introspection:

I like everything about this list but items 4 and 5. I am comfortable working on my own as an expert in this company, but will want to know who's paying the bill and who evaluates my work. I need to know upfront exactly who my client is, so that I can have a useful perspective on my work. From what I can tell now, this seems like the kind of project for which the expert role is appropriate. I'll have to think about it some more before I decide whether I'm right for the expert role.

Consulting Checklist for Experts

Instructions: Review this checklist prior to either contracting for this kind of consultant or being this kind of consultant. Place a checkmark next to each item in the checklist that you are prepared to accept. There are constraints and limitations to this kind of consulting; go into it with eyes open.

❏ 1. Experts are often called when something in a company is really bad.

❏ 2. Management often bows out, leaving the consultant on his/her own, but with the manager's delegated authority.

❏ 3. Project accountability rests entirely with the consultant.

❏ 4. Who the client is often becomes a mystery.

❏ 5. Posturing and politicking by staff often occur.

❏ 6. The consultant must be familiar with information sources within the company and with how to get needed resources.

❏ 7. The consultant sets all parameters of the project.

❏ 8. The consultant is expected to fix a problem and depart.

1.9 Organization Charts and Project Diagrams: Example A

Description

The following blank worksheet is for the consultant to draw a graphic representation of the organization in which consulting work will be done. Four examples have been provided to be used as examples or templates.

Why This Tool Is Important

Graphics can help you understand relationships, and relationships are important as you consider whether to pursue a consulting assignment. Graphics can help you develop your right-brain, and that's not a bad thing either. If you take the consulting challenge, refer to your charts from time to time to be sure that, in the height of the analysis frenzy of midconsulting, you haven't overlooked an important connection in your charts.

Example of How to Use This Tool

Four examples are given on this and three consecutive pages of how to use this tool.

Title of Chart: _Official Training Department Organization Chart 1/16/99_

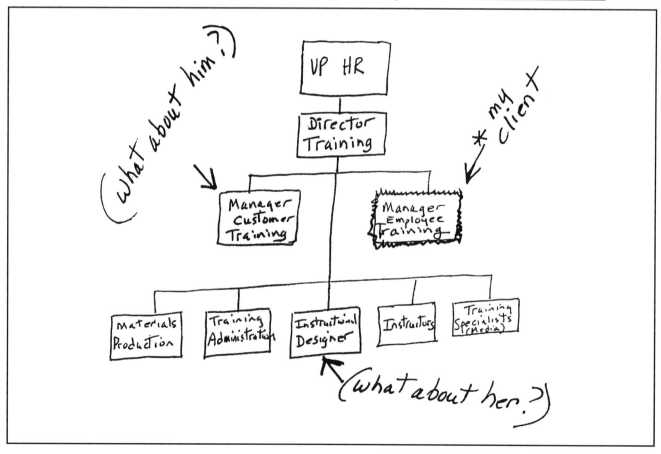

Organization Graphic Worksheet: Example A

Instructions: At contracting time, draw a graphic representation of the organization in which you will be working. Use boxes, circles, arrows, connecting lines, dotted lines, broken lines—whatever graphic devices you determine represent the relationships that will be essential to your success. Consider the organization as a whole—teams, processes, and individuals. Use any and all structures and functions you need. From time to time during your engagement, refer to your charts to verify your original analysis. Make changes as appropriate. Construct as many charts as you find useful.

Title of Chart: _____

1.9 Organization Charts and Project Diagrams: Example B

Description

The following blank worksheet is for the consultant to draw a graphic representation of the organization in which consulting work will be done.

Why This Tool Is Important

Graphics can help you understand relationships, and relationships are important as you consider whether to pursue a consulting assignment. Graphics can help you develop your right-brain, and that's not a bad thing either. If you take the consulting challenge, refer to your charts from time to time to be sure that, in the height of the analysis frenzy of midconsulting, you haven't overlooked an important connection in your charts.

Example of How to Use This Tool

Title of Chart: _Roles Adopted by Key Players 1/16/99_

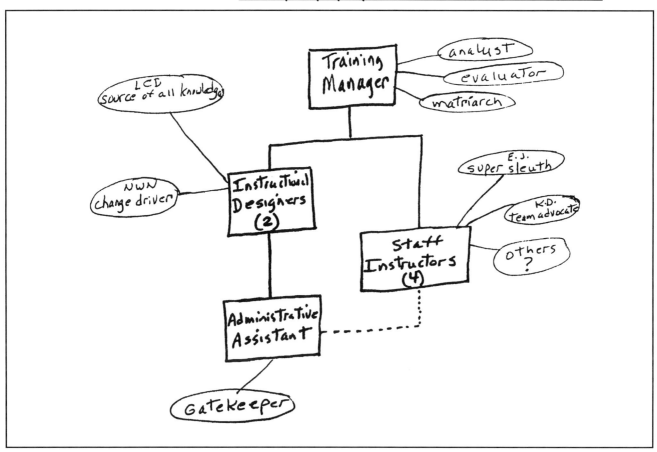

Organization Graphic Worksheet: Example B

Instructions: At contracting time, draw a graphic representation of the organization in which you will be working. Use boxes, circles, arrows, connecting lines, dotted lines, broken lines—whatever graphic devices you determine represent the relationships that will be essential to your success. Consider the organization as a whole—teams, processes, and individuals. Use any and all structures and functions you need. From time to time during your engagement, refer to your charts to verify your original analysis. Make changes as appropriate. Construct as many charts as you find useful.

Title of Chart: _____

1.9 Organization Charts and Project Diagrams: Example C

Description

The following blank worksheet is for the consultant to draw a graphic representation of the organization in which consulting work will be done.

Why This Tool Is Important

Graphics can help you understand relationships, and relationships are important as you consider whether to pursue a consulting assignment. Graphics can help you develop your right-brain, and that's not a bad thing either. If you take the consulting challenge, refer to your charts from time to time to be sure that, in the height of the analysis frenzy of midconsulting, you haven't overlooked an important connection in your charts.

Example of How to Use This Tool

Title of Chart: _External Influences 1/16/99_

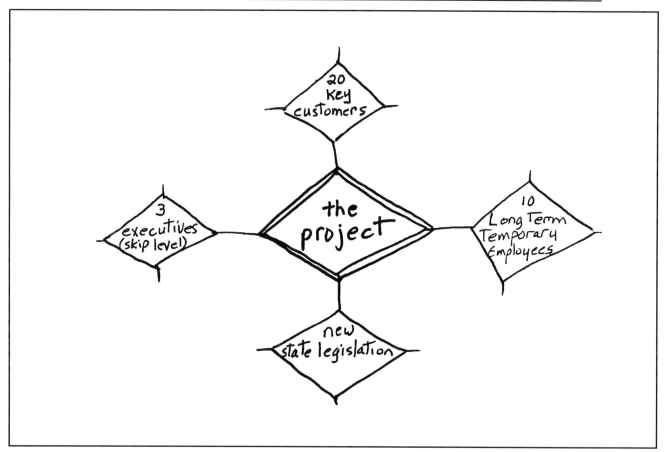

Organization Graphic Worksheet: Example C

Instructions: At contracting time, draw a graphic representation of the organization in which you will be working. Use boxes, circles, arrows, connecting lines, dotted lines, broken lines—whatever graphic devices you determine represent the relationships that will be essential to your success. Consider the organization as a whole—teams, processes, and individuals. Use any and all structures and functions you need. From time to time during your engagement, refer to your charts to verify your original analysis. Make changes as appropriate. Construct as many charts as you find useful.

Title of Chart: _____

1.9 Organization Charts and Project Diagrams: Example D

Description

The following blank worksheet is for the consultant to draw a graphic representation of the organization in which consulting work will be done.

Why This Tool Is Important

Graphics can help you understand relationships, and relationships are important as you consider whether to pursue a consulting assignment. Graphics can help you develop your right-brain, and that's not a bad thing either. Be sure that if you take the consulting challenge, refer to your charts from time to time to be sure that, in the height of the analysis frenzy of midconsulting, you haven't overlooked an important connection in your charts.

Example of How to Use This Tool

Title of Chart: *Process Effects on Project Timeline 1/16/99*

Processes

	1Q	2Q	3Q	4Q
• work flow	X		X	X
• timeliness of R&D results	X	X		
• influence networking	X			
• official written communication		X		X
• monitoring and feedback		X	X	
• beta testing/trials			X	

Organization Graphic Worksheet: Example D

Instructions: At contracting time, draw a graphic representation of the organization in which you will be working. Use boxes, circles, arrows, connecting lines, dotted lines, broken lines—whatever graphic devices you determine represent the relationships that will be essential to your success. Consider the organization as a whole—teams, processes, and individuals. Use any and all structures and functions you need. From time to time during your engagement, refer to your charts to verify your original analysis. Make changes as appropriate. Construct as many charts as you find useful.

Title of Chart: _____

1.10 A New Kind of Job Description

Description

This form specifies the typical categories of a job description. It also includes space to describe any role or roles adopted by/assigned to the individual in a job. Understanding roles is often the secret to supporting performance.

Why This Tool Is Important

This tool merges two types of job description information:

- The *standard information* about job title, supervisor, responsibility for supervision of others, scope and purpose of the job, and job duties.

- The *not-so-standard information* about the role either given to or adopted by the same person.

In performance consulting, determining and dealing with people's roles is as important as dealing with their stated job descriptions. The reason for this is that performance on the job depends on more than skillful deployment of job duties. Roles can give you quicker clues to problem identification and are absolutely essential to assess accurately before you begin to design intervention solutions. The roles individuals have can undermine or advance the implementation of solutions to performance problems.

Example of How to Use This Tool

Take the typical information found in standard job descriptions and supplement it with role information. Here's one example:

	Role
Job title **_Visitor Services Coordinator_**	**_strategist_**
Job title of immediate superior **_Manager of Public Relations_**	**_temperature taker_**
Responsible for others: (#) (job titles of direct reports) **_2. technical assistants_**	• **_monitor_** / **_conscience_**
1. clerical assistant	• **_troubleshooter_**
1. part-time registrar	• **_clown_**
Scope and purpose of job (brief narrative statement)	**_Provides guest services, primarily connected with benchmarking visits._**
Duties of the job	• **_demonstrates products_** • **_schedules visits_** • **_develops brochures_** • **_maintains mailing lists_**

A New Kind of Job Description

Instructions: A performance consultant often needs to have copies of job descriptions of key persons in any organization in which consulting work is done. This job description form has space for roles to be specified in addition to job duties. In today's workplace, roles often determine progress for the organization or project, and they are a key variable in an individual's feeling of accomplishment and job success. Job descriptions don't tell everything a consultant typically needs to know; it is instructive to re-do job descriptions in this format, that is, including each key player's adopted roles too. Expand the form as necessary.

Job title _____ Date _____

Individual holding this job _____

	Role
Job title _____	_____
Job title of immediate superior _____	_____
Responsible for others: (#)	
(job titles of direct reports) _____	_____
_____	_____
_____	_____
_____	_____

Scope and purpose of job
(brief narrative statement)

Duties of the job _____

_____

_____

_____

_____

1.11 Where To Look for Support as You Move toward Performance Consulting

Description

This is a checklist for trainers who have decided to become performance consultants. It suggests places to look for support persons and documents that can facilitate your transition.

Why This Tool Is Important

If you are seriously thinking about being a performance consultant, it's a good idea to line up your resources, both personal and documentary. These transition support resources focus both inwardly on your readiness and outwardly on corporate information that gives a big picture of the company.

Example of How to Use This Tool

This checklist could have been filled out by a trainer looking to become an internal performance consultant.

	Notes
___ 1. Informal internal change agents (individuals) *(Bert)*	
___ 2. Lists of competencies from professional associations *(ISPI)*	
___ 3. Evaluations of past consultants *(ASTD)*	
___ 4. Past consultants' end-of-project reports *(viz. Apex)*	
___ 5. Policies *(all since 1995)*	
___ 6. Procedures manuals	
___ 7. Performance reviews (your own and others)	
___ 8. Corporate annual reports *(viz. '98, '99)*	
___ 9. Corporate goals, vision, and mission statements	
___ 10. Three-year stock performance history and trends	
___ 11. Current business books *(check Robinson, Tobin)*	
___ 12. Professional journals *(viz. Block, Drucker)*	
___ 13. College courses *(executive MBA—B.U.?)*	
___ 14. Websites	

Where to Look for Support as You Move toward Performance Consulting

Instructions: Check as many sources as apply to your situation. Add others as appropriate.

	Notes
___ 1. Informal internal change agents (individuals)	
___ 2. Lists of competencies from professional associations	
___ 3. Evaluations of past consultants	
___ 4. Past consultants' end-of-project reports	
___ 5. Policies	
___ 6. Procedures manuals	
___ 7. Performance reviews (your own and others)	
___ 8. Corporate annual reports	
___ 9. Corporate goals, vision, and mission statements	
___ 10. Three-year stock performance history and trends	
___ 11. Current business books	
___ 12. Professional journals	
___ 13. College courses	
___ 14. Websites	
___ 15. _____	
___ 16. _____	

1.12 What You Have to Do to Get through the Transition from Trainer to Performance Consultant

Description

This graphic suggests the building blocks for moving beyond the role of trainer to that of performance consultant. Constructing these building blocks is the trainer-in-transition's responsibility.

Why This Tool Is Important

Each of these consulting building blocks is an important process that can take you through the transition from trainer to consultant.

Example of How to Use This Tool

Use this as a poster in your office to remind yourself of these consulting building blocks. These are the ways in which you will make a successful transition from training to consulting. In this example, you've starred five blocks that are especially important for your own situation as project opportunities develop. In consulting projects, monitoring, feedback, and use of feedback are critical in getting off to a good start; so is delivering value to your client—that is, value as perceived by the client. Last of all, promote success by networking and ultimately expanding your influence until you feel thoroughly comfortable in the new role.

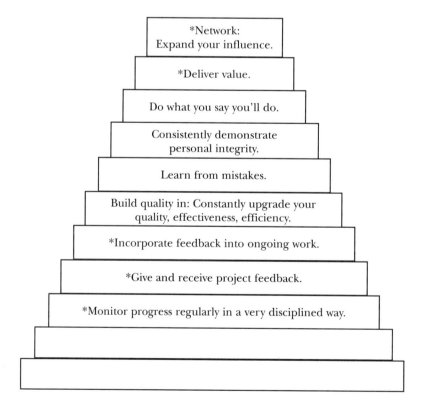

What You Have to Do to Get through the Transition from Trainer to Performance Consultant

Instructions: Use this as a poster in your office as a reminder of how to build transition support. Start at the bottom.

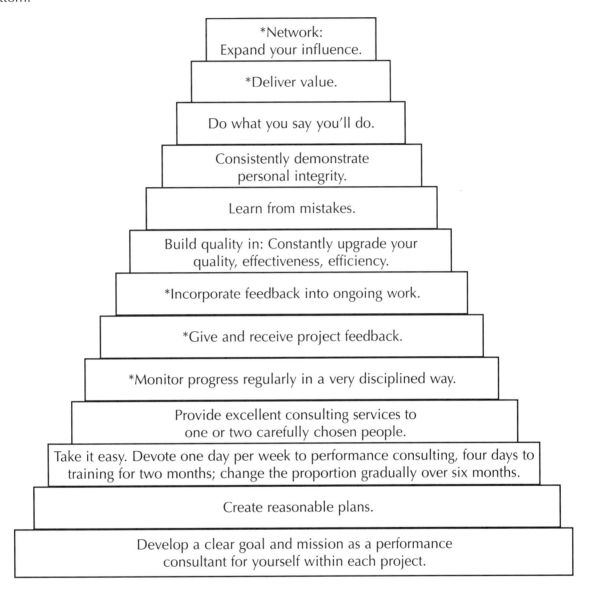

*Network:
Expand your influence.

*Deliver value.

Do what you say you'll do.

Consistently demonstrate
personal integrity.

Learn from mistakes.

Build quality in: Constantly upgrade your
quality, effectiveness, efficiency.

*Incorporate feedback into ongoing work.

*Give and receive project feedback.

*Monitor progress regularly in a very disciplined way.

Provide excellent consulting services to
one or two carefully chosen people.

Take it easy. Devote one day per week to performance consulting, four days to
training for two months; change the proportion gradually over six months.

Create reasonable plans.

Develop a clear goal and mission as a performance
consultant for yourself within each project.

1.13 Three-Month Timeline for Transition Planning

Description

This timeline is for the individual trainer who intends to become a performance consultant, either internal or external.

Why This Tool Is Important

The primary discipline of consulting is self-management. You must find ways to assess your own strengths and weaknesses. Tools like this one can help you maintain the discipline you'll need to keep yourself at peak performance. Consider transition planning in areas that represent gaps in your own ability to perform as a consultant.

Example of How to Use This Tool

These items represent gaps in performance that can be corrected during the time you have specified as your transition time.

Month 1.0

5. Complete e-mail directory by 3/7.

6. Be sure personal files are complete re: models of job analysis (D of L, apprenticeship, Mager, etc.)

Month 1.5

7. Get Bob to videotape me practicing interviewing skills with Jeffrey at the clinic; review tape the following week.

8. (Don't forget spring vacation. Allow 10 days.)

Month 2.0

9. Before 4/15 also get somebody to critique my questioning skills (use at least four different recognizable skills).

10. Spend one week now to assemble library on business writing. Check Borders, amazon.com, Corner Books.

Month 2.5

11. Get NWN to explain reading between the lines in corporate annual reports. Take him to lunch the week of 5/3.

Month 3.0

12.

Month 3.5

13.

Three-Month Timeline for Transition Planning

Instructions: List the skills/knowledge you must get more of to begin work as a performance consultant. This timeline is purposely short; it is intended to make you refocus your work orientation in a very disciplined way. Extend the timeline onto longer paper or a flipchart to allow greater detail.

These are just some of the major areas for skill and knowledge development for performance consulting, in which you need specific plans to effectively make the transition from where you are now to where you want to be: business finances, descriptive statistics, interviewing skills, giving and receiving feedback, writing with clarity (objectives, goals, procedures, reports), job and task analysis, organizational analysis skills, evaluation methods and procedures. Consider transition planning in these and other areas that represent gaps in your own ability to perform as a consultant.

_____ Month 1.0

_____ Month 1.5

_____ Month 2.0

_____ Month 2.5

_____ Month 3.0

_____ Month 3.5

1.14 Chart of Differences between Good Service and Good Contracting

Description

This checklist chart shows the basic elements of good service and good contracting, with an intent of highlighting the differences between them.

Why This Tool Is Important

Essential during the transition from trainer to performance consultant is to differentiate between service and contracting. A frequent criticism of trainers is that they are stuck in a service mentality, that they are accustomed to respond and not to initiate, that they are too concerned with the effect of the moment and have little vision of future effect, that they typically say "how high?" when a manager says "jump" rather than question whether "jump" is the right thing to do. Trainers are accused of typically seeing "trees" and not "forests." Folks may say that these ways of thinking and acting are fine demonstrations of providing good service. Good contracting, however, requires different kinds of thinking and action. Good contracting is the beginning of good consulting. Use this chart as a self-assessment device.

Example of How to Use This Tool

Good Service (Training)	Good Contracting (Consulting)
2. All of one's "need to know" plus some "nice to know."	2. Specified items only.

Item 2 in Tool 1.14 is perhaps the most illustrative of the change in thinking that's required of a trainer who becomes a consultant. It also causes trainers perhaps the most grief as they attempt to defend what they perceive as their good work. Trainers today are often criticized for inserting too many "nice to know" elements of content into courses; off-the-shelf and generic, vendor-provided courses very often are loaded with "nice-to-know" content—to the great consternation of trainees and managers who pay for them. This argument about what a trainer often has in the past perceived as value in a course has of late given way to the "just-in-time" movement in training design. Trainers who persist in teaching nice-to-know material have a particularly hard time as consultants contracting for specified items only. In consulting, both parties know that fees are based on person-hours of time; contracting demands a much tighter adherence to the specified needs of the project.

Chart of Differences between Good Service and Good Contracting

Instructions: Use this self-assessment device as you make the transition between trainer and performance consultant. Check off the items in which you need more understanding or better skills; then pursue these gaps in your preparation before you give up work as a trainer to begin work as a performance consultant.

Good Service (Training)	*Good Contracting (Consulting)*
1. Effective response.	___ 1. Mutual consent to contract.
2. All of one's "need to know" plus some "nice to know."	___ 2. Specified items only.
3. Content of high value per the service request.	___ 3. Content of high value per the items in the contract.
4. Process that supports smooth organizational functioning.	___ 4. Collaborative planning and problem identification/solving.
5. Descriptive understanding of the request for service.	___ 5. Consideration of each party's expectations and rights.
6. Assertiveness in delivering the service requested.	___ 6. Freedom of access; freedom to innovate.

1.15 How to Establish Credibility as a Consultant

Description

This is a checklist to be used as a reminder of major ways in which to gain consulting credibility. It highlights the personal and professional behaviors by which consultants are typically selected, retained, and rehired.

Why This Tool Is Important

Establishing credibility as a trainer entails very different processes than those for establishing credibility as a consultant. This tool gives you ten key points about consultant credibility. Refer to it each time you seek a new consulting job as a reminder and a refresher.

Example of How to Use This Tool

This might be one of your self-assessments as a reminder to pay particular attention to these four items in one of your potential consulting jobs:

____   **3.** Use your network of personal professional connections.

____   **4.** Demonstrate solid content information.

____   **7.** Accept responsibility.

____   **10.** Act with integrity.

Items 3, 4, 7, and 10 are often particularly troublesome to a person who is getting into consulting for the first time. Item 3 presents a problem to trainers because trainers are not used to having to network: trainers do not typically focus outwardly, especially if the organization in which they are located is a cost center, not a profit center. Items 4 and 10 are related: Often someone new to consulting is tempted to "weasel word" their writing and their speaking; often it seems the thing to do to adopt the latest jargon without an understanding of its application to the client's situation. Clients quickly see through self-centeredness, sham, and sales pitch. Item 7 is critically important: consulting is a business that is full of variables. Mistakes and errors are inevitable; the wise person learns from mistakes and accepts responsibility for them.

How to Establish Credibility as a Consultant

Instructions: Use this checklist each time you decide to seek a consulting contract.

____ 1. Demonstrate your own competent performance, past or present.

____ 2. Prove that you are a continuous learner.

____ 3. Use your network of personal professional connections.

____ 4. Demonstrate solid content information.

____ 5. Be able to choose and use a wide variety of process interventions.

____ 6. Know yourself: your own needs and wants from consulting, be able to articulate your values, know your preferred working styles

____ 7. Accept responsibility.

____ 8. Be fiscally accountable.

____ 9. Provide complete, accurate, relevant, necessary and sufficient information.

____ 10. Act with integrity.

1.16 How to Adapt Elements of Good Training to Good Consulting

Description

This diagram illustrates various kinds of creative behaviors that can be used to adapt good training skills and practices to those required for consulting.

Why This Tool Is Important

This tool helps you think creatively about consulting behaviors. At the same time it reinforces what you know as your own good training behaviors and differentiates each from the other.

Creative Behaviors

alter   arrange   ask   change combine defend design
express *feel* find generalize guess modify
paraphrase predict question rearrange reconstruct regroup
rename restate restructure revise rewrite scan
simplify simulate *synthesize* value vary

Good Training	*Good Consulting*
1. I focus on individual learners.	•
2. I have excellent presentation skills.	•
3. I *memorize* well and never lose my place.	• I have good intuition and can synthesize information from many sources.

Example of How to Use This Tool

This is an example of a conversation you might have with yourself as you try to see the differences between good training and good consulting.

Good training #3. *If I apply the creative behaviors of "feel" and "synthesize" to my training behavior of "memorize," I might be able to abandon my need to use the controlling behavior of reliance on memory. It is, after all, a rather rigid ability, and not exactly indicative of an open attitude toward unexpressed or unknown client needs. It probably would be much better to sense the client environment and aim ultimately to be able to synthesize what I see, hear, and feel in my gut.*

How to Adapt Elements of Good Training to Good Consulting

Instructions: List for yourself the characteristics of your personal training behavior and style that you consider good. Then refer one by one to the items listed in "creative behaviors," referencing each creative behavior to your strengths. Apply one or more creative behavior to each listed item with the objective of broadening your scope, demonstrating business sense, having a client orientation, exhibiting process flexibility, or any other behavior you have come to understand as good consulting practice.

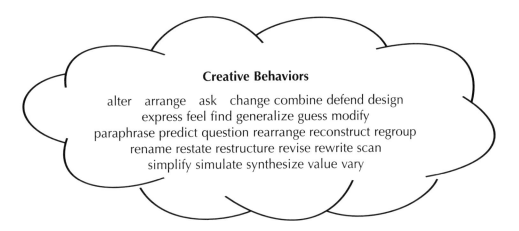

Creative Behaviors

alter   arrange   ask   change combine defend design
express feel find generalize guess modify
paraphrase predict question rearrange reconstruct regroup
rename restate restructure revise rewrite scan
simplify simulate synthesize value vary

Good Training	*Good Consulting*
1. _____	• _____
2. _____	• _____
3. _____	• _____
4. _____	• _____
5. _____	• _____
6. _____	• _____
7. _____	• _____
8. _____	• _____

Chapter 2

Human Performance Technology in Plain English

In this chapter you'll find tools that describe human performance technology and explanations about how to use them. This chapter's goal is to talk in plain English about human performance—defining terms, clarifying concepts, and explaining how performance technology is different from training. You will be ready to learn from Chapter 2 if you have begun to change your thinking from that of a trainer to a consultant by assimilating the information in Chapter 1.

In this chapter you'll see the differences between training/learning and performing, and you'll find a host of examples and elaborative material about the field of human performance. We will also compare and contrast training with performance consulting.

This chapter is meant to give you a comprehensive rundown of the important terms, concepts, and ideas about "performance"—all the good words you'll need to be successful as a performance consultant. Chapter 2 is full of most of what you'll ever need to know about performance. Take what you need from it, and don't be intimidated by how much information is here. Learning the sometimes confusing new vocabulary may be the hardest part!

While we give you more than enough to think about, we also give you plenty of help in working your way through Chapter 2. In this chapter we provide 15 tools and instructions for their use. With these, you can quickly understand the parameters of performance and prepare yourself to successfully use a particular tool to enhance human performance, either as an internal staff member or as an external performance consultant. A special feature of this chapter is the "Human Performance Glossary" of the most familiar terms in the field, presented for easy reference at the end of the chapter.

Tools in Chapter 2

2.1 Comparison Chart between Learning and Performance

Description

This chart contains the key points of difference between learning and performance.

Why This Tool Is Important

Trainers come from a training/learning perspective. The field of performance is broader than learning, although learning can certainly affect performance, as can the lack of learning. This tool is important because it helps you see quickly the differences between learning and performance. Review it anytime you need a quick refresher. As Gloria Gery, performance guru of electronic performance support systems (EPSS), said recently, "When you support performance, people learn while they're doing. When you support learning—well, who knows what they'll learn?" (*Training Magazine,* February 1998, p. 63). This tool is important because trainers who want to "get into performance" have to be very clear from the beginning about the differences between training/learning and performance.

Example of How to Use This Tool

This tool can be especially helpful as a reminder before you meet a prospective consulting client for the first time, or as background prior to your drafting your first consulting contract.

Comparison Chart between Learning and Performance

Instructions: Review the points side by side so that you understand the comparisons.

Learning	*Performance*
• Inside focus—what goes on in a person's head	• Outside focus—what happens in the work environment
• Increase in an individual's knowledge, skills, and/or attitudes	• Demonstration of a person's competencies applied to work
• Result of the confluence of mental constructs, generally consciously designed to achieve a positive intellectual change	• Result of action against behavioral standards
• Dependent on various personality styles and preferences	• Dependent on removing obstacles from the work environment
• Measured against objectives for learning	• Measured against objectives for doing

2.2 Relationship between Performance Technology, Performance Enhancement, and Performance Consulting

Description

This matrix shows you the similarities and differences between the terms "performance technology," "performance enhancement," and "performance consulting."

Why This Tool Is Important

In the heat of your enthusiasm for becoming a performance consultant instead of a trainer—or in the frustration at your present situation—you rush into your new field and adopt its jargon without a clear understanding of the meanings of the field's favorite terms. One of the worst mistakes a consultant can make is to confuse a prospective client because of your own inadequate understanding.

Example of How to Use This Tool

Use this tool as is, or expand it by adding your own definitions, as you seek to further your understanding of the field. Consider expanding the matrix both horizontally and vertically by adding to it. Here are some other performance terms you might want to add to the categories across the top: performance analysis, performance appraisal, performance deficiency, performance goal, performance objective, performance support. The more you read, the more related terms you'll uncover. The field is currently full of persons—academics as well as business persons—who are trying to make a name for themselves in "performance;" each has a slightly different angle to promote, and you'll find many different definitions and variations on a theme. The Human Performance Glossary at the end of this chapter is designed to help you further sort out some of these definitions. This matrix-type chart is another way of presenting identifying and defining information; use it in any way that you find helpful.

Use this tool before you meet your prospective client. Use it as a practice aid, by referring to it as you role-play with yourself in practice dialogue with a fake client. Practice using the term with the precise meaning you intend, so that you get used to hearing yourself choose and use the best term to convey what you want to convey. Practice by writing, by talking into a mirror or to an imaginary client, by speaking into an audio tape recorder, or by setting up a stationary video camera on yourself as you speak. With so many related terms out there these days, practice is the only way you'll gain the confidence to assure that you can use the correct term for your client situation.

Relationship between Performance Technology, Performance Enhancement, and Performance Consulting

Instructions: Refer to this chart before you engage in conversation or writing about performance. Use it to help yourself clarify and refine your understanding of the variations and dimensions of performance. Cells in the matrix are blank if the characteristic is generally not shared in common. An "X" indicates the presence of the characteristic.

Performance Characteristic	Performance Technology	Performance Enhancement	Performance Consulting
1. Systematic approach to improving performance	X	X	X
2. Inclusion of the organizational environment	X		X
3. Problem identification and solution finding			X
4. Dependent on feedback	X		X
5. Focuses on self-control and personal mastery		X	
6. Directly tied to performance objectives		X	
7. Satisfying a client is the primary primary goal			X
8.			
9.			
10.			

2.3 Variables to Watch Out for in a Consulting Assignment

Description

This is a checklist of the many considerations you must pay attention to as you set the parameters for a performance consulting assignment.

Why This Tool Is Important

This tool helps you expand your thinking to include many different variables before you design a performance consulting engagement. You have to remember that when a prospective client approaches you to help solve a performance problem, the client is driven by a "trigger" problem, which may or may not be the underlying problem that needs solving. As the consultant, you have to be able to think broadly to discover what could be many causes of the performance problem behind the trigger driving the client to ask for your help.

This tool is based on the early work of Thomas Gilbert (1978), the pioneer in the field of human performance technology, and of the American Society for Training and Development (ASTD), who published the *ASTD Models for Human Performance Improvement* by William J. Rothwell (1996).

Example of How to Use This Tool

Use this tool as a job aid as you prepare for the design work involved in a performance consulting assignment. It is especially useful as you enter the contracting process, so that you don't overlook any contingency as you prepare a consulting contract. It is also useful as you prepare talking points prior to meetings with your potential client.

Variables to Watch Out for in a Consulting Assignment

Instructions: Use this as a checklist of variables that apply to your own particular consulting situation. Review the list item by item before you scope out your project and before you meet with a client. Use it to review the possibilities in performance consulting so that you remember to think of all contingencies as you approach the design of a consulting job.

- ❏   1. Current performance
- ❏   2. Desired performance
- ❏   3. Definition of the gap in performance
- ❏   4. Motivation
- ❏   5. Incentives
- ❏   6. Rewards
- ❏   7. Objectives
- ❏   8. Expectations
- ❏   9. Bias
- ❏ 10. Punishment
- ❏ 11. Feedback
- ❏ 12. Intellectual competencies
- ❏ 13. Physical competencies
- ❏ 14. Emotional competencies
- ❏ 15. Job skills
- ❏ 16. Job knowledge
- ❏ 17. Data
- ❏ 18. Information
- ❏ 19. Time
- ❏ 20. Financial resources/support
- ❏ 21. Procedures
- ❏ 22. Pay
- ❏ 23. Benefits
- ❏ 24. Tools and equipment
- ❏ 25. Work environment
- ❏ 26. Training/career development
- ❏ 27. Supervision
- ❏ 28. Management
- ❏ 29. Staffing
- ❏ 30. Business goals

2.4 Models for Troubleshooting and Problem Solving

Description

These four models contain common elements of problem solving.

Why This Tool Is Important

The performance consultant's primary work task is to be a competent problem solver. This means having an understanding of how to go about looking for trouble without getting into trouble yourself. This tool gives you a basic perspective on models for problem solving—ideas that form the foundation for developing competency as a problem solver.

Example of How to Use This Tool

Problem-solving models usually have some commonalities:

- A *problem description phase,* in which the client initiates the first cues.

- A *search for solutions* with associated mental constructs to name and prioritize the solution options.

- A *solution choice and implementation phase,* including monitoring, testing, and providing feedback.

Consultant skills of both analysis and synthesis are required for effective problem solving, as are skills of both convergent and divergent thinking.

Problem solvers are encouraged to identify the type of problem being specified:

- The *puzzle problem,* in which the many finite pieces are out there and simply have to be located and assembled in the right order.

- The *logical or mathematical problem,* in which there is only one acceptable correct solution.

- The *situated problem,* sometimes called a "creative problem," in which many variables affect the definition of the problem and in which many solutions could be suggested.

It is this last kind of problem that performance consultants most often address. [See David H. Jonassen, in Smith (1998) for more detail about types of problems.]

The literature on creativity and innovation can be helpful in your learning to be a better problem solver. Creative thinking requires flexibility of approach; a demonstrated competency for self-regulation or "metacognition" ability; ability to visualize and brainstorm; and a set of skills in mental manipulations involving techniques such as means–ends analysis, working backwards, making inferences, part-whole analysis, applying rules and scripts, using metaphor and analogy; seeing the forest as well as the trees; and using simple redefinition techniques such as substitution, refinement, translation, paraphrase, reconstitution, recombination, rewrite, restatement, restructure, and reorganize. David H. Jonassen of Penn State University is currently publishing in academic journals on the topic of problem solving. A 1998 book, *Quality Problem Solving,* by Gerald F. Smith was published by the American Society for Quality (ASQ). Authors from earlier years are Robert Gagne (1996), James Greeno (1977), Alan Newell and Herbert A. Simon (1972), and Alex Osborn (1954). Lawrence Erlbaum Associates, a publisher in Hillsdale, New Jersey, has an extensive publications list in creativity and problem solving. Look for these sources if you need more information about troubleshooting and problem solving.

Models for Troubleshooting and Problem Solving

Instructions: Refer to this page as a refresher as you troubleshoot a client's performance problem and begin planning for solving the problem or problems you identify.

The IDEAL Problem Solver

This model is based on the classic work of Alan Newell and Herbert Simon in using information processing theory and applying it to human problem solving. The IDEAL acronym and mnemonic stands for: **I** = Identifying, **D** = Defining, **E** = Exploring, **A** = Acting, and **L** = Looking Back. It is the simplest process representation of problem solving.

Bransford, J. & Stein, B.S. *The IDEAL Problem Solver.* New York: W.H.Freeman, 1984.

The Huddle

The imagery of the football huddle is a useful trigger to problem solving. Call a huddle of key "players" any time you need to focus on a particular problem. As in the football huddle, don't sit down. Stand shoulder to shoulder facing each other in a circle and strategize the "plays" in solving the problem at hand. Swift and focused action usually follows the huddle on the field; the metaphor can work the same way around the office. Don't be afraid to use techniques like the huddle in your problem-solving efforts.

Nilson, Carolyn. *Team Games for Trainers.* New York: McGraw-Hill, 1993, p. 301.

Ill-Structured Problems and Well-Structured Problems

It is useful to first define problems as either ill-structured or well-structured, according to the recent work of David H. Jonassen of Penn State University. Professor Jonassen suggests that most workplace problems are of the ill-structured type, requiring a set of *learning* skills that are framed within constructivist educational theories. His long paper, referenced below, details the relationships between problem solving and learning to be a problem solver.

Jonassen, David H. "Instructional Design Models for Well-Structured and Ill-Structured Problem-Solving Learning Outcomes," in *Educational Technology Research and Development,* v.45 n.1, 1997, p. 65–94.

What? Why? and What If?

A very basic way to think about problem solving is to think in terms of the three simple questions—what? why? what if?—in that order. Answers to the question what? provide definitions and descriptions. Answers to the question why? provide insights and analysis. Answers to the question what if? lead you into generation of options for solutions and to verification of your choices. Problem finding, solution finding, and acceptance finding are the most basic frames of problem solving.

2.5 Steps in Analytical Thinking

Description

Follow these steps as you decode performance problems, that is, break down larger sets of information into their component parts.

Why This Tool Is Important

Analysis is the first phase in both instructional system design and in performance consulting. Trainers recognize this phase by its "training" terminology as front-end analysis or needs assessment. Analysis is characterized by a rather narrow set of skills whose purpose is to break down a complicated set of information into its component parts in order to more easily figure out how to deal with it. Some typical skills of analysis include arranging, categorizing, classifying, contrasting, deducing, differentiating, distinguishing, sequencing, and summarizing. Skills of analysis are often associated with "left-brain" capacities and with logical and procedural thinking. Analysis is unlike problem solving, which includes much broader and more "creative" skills.

Analysis is the favorite starting place for those who believe in a systems approach to organizational life. In such a belief orientation, the organizational system is generally seen as being composed of inputs, processes or throughputs, and outputs. Good analysis helps people see the beginnings of learning loops or problem-solving loops that then proceed through design, implementation, and evaluation and back to a fresh analysis at the start of a new loop.

Example of How to Use This Tool

The danger for performance consultants in analysis is the danger of being too specific too fast. Analysis that is too hasty can identify the wrong problems and cost you and the client an unfortunate waste of resources. Save the specificity and focus of analysis for the time when you have finished the broader organizational assessment and have consciously employed skills of divergent thinking, encouraging "big picture" thinking, helping people discover analogies, and other investigations into people's motivational and emotional experiences at work.

Follow these steps of analysis when you are ready to zero in on a problem.

Steps in Analytical Thinking

Instructions: Review this job aid prior to any operation of your consulting project that requires you to exercise your skills of analytical thinking. Remember that the purpose of analysis is to clarify.

1. Define objectives for this analysis.

2. Determine the project context to be studied.

3. Decide how corporate values/goals/mission relate to your chosen context.

4. Identify all individuals who have a stake in solving this performance problem.

5. Collect data from these individuals.

6. Define one or more performance problems and prioritize them.

7. Construct a system representation of the performance problem(s) using graphics (e.g., flow-charts, maps, decision trees, fishbone diagrams, etc.).

8. Specify predictions about problem-solving outcomes; specify tools and plans for successful outcomes.

9. Verify and test the correctness of your analysis with stakeholders.

2.6 Characteristics of Good Performance

Description

This is a list of some of the most common characteristics of good human performance. Look around the organization to find those who exhibit these positive characteristics; expect high performance from them.

Why This Tool Is Important

This is the first in a series of four lists detailing the traits and causes associated with human performance. As you begin performance consulting, you must get these items straight in your mind. The four lists are presented consecutively, for you to compare and contrast to further your understanding.

This list helps you to identify the positive effects of human performance, that is, the consequences that follow performing well. Studying how the good performers do their jobs can help you design interventions that help others perform at the same level.

Example of How to Use This Tool

Imagine that you are engaging in your first performance consulting opportunity. You know that you have to "get your arms around" exactly what performance means in this organization. You want to be sure that you are distinguishing between learning and performance. As you read down the list of characteristics of good human performance, Tool 2.6, you quickly get a clearer picture of what to look for in the organization. You can use this list to point you in the direction of excellent performers. Knowing the characteristics of good performance can help you correctly diagnose performance problems and ultimately design interventions that help to improve employee performance.

Characteristics of Good Performance

Instructions: Review this list as you begin to diagnose human performance problems. Chances are that persons who exhibit these positive characteristics are the high performers in an organization. Use this list in conjunction with the three other lists, Tools 2.7, 2.8, and 2.9.

___ Incremental improvement over time

___ Job satisfaction

___ Professional visibility

___ Recognition and rewards

___ Adaptability

___ Willingness to lead

___ Willingness to teach, mentor, coach

___ Physical and emotional health

2.7 Characteristics of Poor Performance

Description

This is a list of some of the most common characteristics of poor human performance. Look around the organization to find folks who exhibit these characteristics; expect poor performance from them.

Why This Tool Is Important

This is the second in a series of four lists detailing the traits and causes associated with human performance. As you begin performance consulting, you must get these items straight in your mind. The four lists are presented consecutively, for you to compare and contrast to further your understanding.

This list helps you to identify the characteristics of poor performance. Studying poor performers can help you identify organizational structures, disincentives, bureaucracy, etc., that are contributing to poor performance. This helps you design interventions to improve the organizational factors that hurt employee performance.

Example of How to Use This Tool

Again, imagine that you are engaging in your first performance consulting opportunity. You know that you have to "get your arms around" exactly what good and bad performance looks like in this organization. As you read down the list of negative consequences of human performance (Tool 2.7), you quickly get a clearer picture of what to look for, i.e., the characteristics of poor performance. You can use this list to point you in the direction of people who are underperforming. Examining the characteristics of their performance can help you correctly diagnose performance problems elsewhere in the organization, and ultimately design interventions that help to improve their performance.

Characteristics of Poor Performance

Instructions: Review this list as you begin to diagnose human performance problems. Chances are that persons who display these characteristics are the low or mediocre performers in an organization. Use this list in conjunction with the three other lists, Tools 2.6, 2.8, and 2.9.

___ Atrophied skills

___ Increased mistakes

___ Lack of communication

___ Unmet expectations

___ Lack of commitment

___ Low self-esteem

___ Lack of influence

___ Job plateauing/ lack of career advancement

___ Layoff

2.8 Causes of Good Performance

Description

This is a list of some of the most common causes of good human performance. Each of these items can show up in a performance needs analysis and lead to accurate problem diagnosis.

Why This Tool Is Important

This is the third in a series of four lists detailing the consequences and causes associated with human performance. As you begin performance consulting, you must get these items straight in your mind. The four lists are presented consecutively, for you to compare and contrast to further your understanding.

This list helps you to identify the types of causes of positive human performance, that is, the places for you to look in order to find out the reasons why certain individuals and organizations can and do perform well. Thorough analysis of any of these areas can yield a wealth of information about what works in an organization and why.

Example of How to Use This Tool

You have now gotten to the point in your thinking about performance consulting that you need to ferret out the causes of performance that is demonstrably good. This situation can typically occur during early conversations with your prospective client, as you ask probing questions to define the performance problems behind the "trigger" problem. This situation also typically occurs as you do a formal performance needs analysis, looking to define the gaps between actual performance and optimal performance. The search for causes is part of the early work of performance consulting.

Causes of Good Performance

Instructions: Review this list as you begin to diagnose human performance problems. This list can be especially useful as you prepare to analyze performance needs. Use this list in conjunction with the three other lists, Tools 2.6, 2.7, and 2.9.

___ Necessary and sufficient data

___ Complete information

___ Procedures that work

___ Realistic policies

___ Reasonable and valid skill standards

___ Useful feedback

___ Customer satisfaction

___ Freedom to learn from mistakes

___ Adequate training

___ Challenging work

___ Fair compensation

___ Respect

___ Opportunities for participation, empowerment

___ Ability to be a continuous learner

2.9 Causes of Poor Performance

Description

This is a list of some of the most common causes of poor human performance. Each of these items can be typically found during a performance needs analysis and problem diagnosis. Together they represent the range of variables typically detailed in models of human performance technology.

Why This Tool Is Important

This is the last in a series of four lists detailing the traits and causes of human performance. As you begin performance consulting, you must get these items straight in your mind. The four lists are presented consecutively, for you to compare and contrast to further your understanding.

This list helps you to identify the types of causes of negative human performance, that is, the places for you to look to find out why certain individuals and organizations perform poorly. Thorough analysis of any of these areas can yield a wealth of information about the causes of mediocre and poor performance. This list can give you insights into preventable personal and organizational causes of poor performance.

Example of How to Use This Tool

You have now gotten to the point in your thinking about performance consulting that you need to ferret out the causes of poor performance. This situation can typically occur during early conversations with your prospective client, as you ask probing questions to help define the performance problems behind the "trigger" problem. This situation also typically occurs as you do a formal performance needs analysis, looking to define the gaps between actual performance and optimal performance. The search for causes is part of the early work of performance consulting.

Causes of Poor Performance

Instructions: Review this list as you begin to diagnose human performance problems. This list can be especially useful as you prepare to analyze performance needs. Use this list in conjunction with the three other lists, Tools 2.6, 2.7, and 2.8.

___ Unattainable objectives

___ Wide gaps between actual and optimal performance

___ Inadequate training

___ Inadequate resources

___ Lack of support

___ Broken or outdated equipment

___ Lack of knowledge and skills

___ Bad timing

___ Anger, fear, depression, out-of-control emotions

___ Inflexibility

___ Lack of self-regulation ability

___ Unethical behavior

___ Unsafe or hostile work environment

___ Unclear business goals

2.10 How to Determine What Is versus What Should Be

Description

This is a checklist of considerations as you begin to plan to study the performance gaps during a performance needs analysis.

Why This Tool Is Important

Analysis of performance gaps is an important process of performance consulting. It is unique to performance consulting, and it differs from training needs analysis because it uses a broader approach involving whole organizational influences. In training, you analyze the gaps of an individual in knowledge, skills, or attitudes required for the job, and you close the gaps with training in those areas of deficiency. It is important as you think about performance gaps that you constantly remind yourself not to act like a trainer and focus too narrowly. Learn to accept training as only one small gap-filling strategy.

Example of How to Use This Tool

Review this checklist item by item before you attempt to identify and define performance gaps. Remember too that you need to collaborate with the client in this process, and that the client needs to collaborate with you—a 50/50 deal. Don't get trapped into the trainer mentality of doing what the manager said to do.

How to Determine What Is versus What Should Be

Instructions: Use this checklist as a design tool to help you determine an approach to analyzing the gap in performance, that is, what is versus what should be. (Detailed steps follow in Chapters 5 and 6.) Use this checklist to first expand and then to focus your thinking about gap analysis.

___   1. Distinguish between wants and needs.

___   2. Consider organizational, team, and individual needs.

___   3. State clearly the desired performance (what should be).

___   4. State clearly the actual performance (what is).

___   5. Match up what the client says the problem is and what you see as the performance gap; compare, contrast, break into subproblems.

___   6. Decide where you can correlate the defined gaps with stated company goals, mission, business plans.

___   7. Guard against being simply reactive to the client's statements.

___   8. Make no assumptions and accept no assumptions that training is the answer to performance needs or the way to close the gaps.

___   9. Guard against acceptance of national surveys or journalistic opinions as valid input to your analysis of gaps; design your own gap-identifying data collection instruments and processes.

___ 10. Look for consequences and causes in the internal capacities of individuals and in the work environment that surrounds individuals.

___ 11. Look for gaps due to data, resources, motivation, knowledge and skill, and physical, intellectual, and emotional capacity.

___ 12. Be proactive in questioning, in listening, in communicating, in designing, and in planning; identify gaps early in your consulting assignment.

___ 13. Don't ignore the gap assessment; take the time to do this process carefully.

2.11 Chart of Competencies

Description

This four-section chart categorizes worker competencies in the areas of physical, intellectual, emotional, and values and beliefs

Why This Tool Is Important

Competency goes along with performance. Competency is to performance what skill is to training. Both competency and performance suggest broader relationships than do skill and training. A *competency* is an on-the-job behavior representing an internal capability of an individual, often the result of accumulated experience, intuition, and the integration of past learnings. It is resident in a person, and it enables a person to perform. High performers have many competencies that come together. High performers have more than job skills or high levels of training. Competence is more than the effects of learning.

Having said all this, the job of a performance consultant is to figure out exactly what competencies workers in this company must have if they are to be high performers. Often the performance consultant backs into this by determining what competencies are lacking or what present obstacles are preventing competent behavior from being realized. The major consulting task is to devise ways to assess competency. This tool is a place to start.

Example of How to Use This Tool

Competency assessment is an in-depth analysis. This tool is only the first place to start; it is useful as a way to think about breadth in analysis. It is useful for the performance consultant who has just come out of the disciplines and models of training to begin to understand the dimensions of competence and its relationship to performance. More tools for depth analysis are given in Chapters 5 and 6, as the steps in performance consulting are presented.

Use this tool early in performance consulting, when you are faced with having to align corporate or business goals with the individuals presently in positions to do the work of accomplishing the goals. You are faced with a need to find an analysis framework as you continue to scope out the nature of your consulting project.

Use this tool also as an example to share with your client if the client has had a hard time articulating to what traits or characteristics are valued or sought. It can be used as a "talking points" sheet to lead you into collaborative discussion about competencies. This tool can help you establish parameters for further work in competency assessment.

Chart of Competencies

Instructions: Use this chart to analyze the totality of the worker's capacity to perform. Add or delete items to customize the chart to your situation.

PHYSICAL

___ Speed and accuracy of response to stimulus	___ Timing
___ Reliability of spatial orientation	___ Consistency
___ Strength	___ Neatness
___ Muscle flexibility	___ _____
___ General health	___ _____
___ Reliability of pattern repetition	___ _____

INTELLECTUAL

___ Knowledge of job content	___ Synthesis
___ Oral communication	___ Evaluation
___ Written communication	___ Organization
___ Can learn from mistakes	___ Planning
___ Decision making	___ Logic, mathematics
___ Analysis	___ _____

EMOTIONAL

___ Assertiveness	___ Enthusiasm
___ Sense of self	___ Kindness
___ Self-confidence	___ Respect
___ Pride in work	___ Generosity, sharing
___ Can deal with ambiguity	___ _____
___ Has a long fuse	___ _____
___ Has a range of emotions	___ _____

VALUES AND BELIEFS

___ Loyal	___ Objective
___ Moral	___ Accepts responsibility
___ Unbiased	___ Courageous
___ Principled	___ Honest
___ Follows rules	___ Trustworthy
___ Independent	___ _____

2.12 Rewards Checklist

Description

This checklist suggests the most common financial and nonfinancial rewards given to workers for good performance.

Why This Tool Is Important

Like motivation, rewards represent an important foundation of human performance. Like motivation, rewards are largely a personal affair, that is, uniquely meaningful to an individual. Like motivation, rewards also have a social dimension. These two aspects of rewards make them important to performance and to performance consultants. Rewards influence performance; the more carefully rewards are matched to individual preferences, the more likely the individual is to want to perform better to qualify for more rewards. Wise performance consultants examine the rewards practices in a company to determine their influences on performance, especially on future performance.

Rewards follow performance; they reinforce the results of performance and encourage more of the same. Individuals who are rewarded and who believe that the corporate culture and environment will continue to allow them to be rewarded can be expected to perform at high levels.

Example of How to Use This Tool

Use this tool as a reminder to search beneath the surface of rewards practices at the client company. Rewards have an effect on performance; the lack of rewards or withdrawal of rewards also has an effect on performance. Take the time to interview many individuals regarding their own perceptions about rewards. You'll be amazed at the motivational effect the right reward can have on individual performance.

Rewards Checklist

Instructions: Use this list as only a beginning, as a reminder of some of the most common rewards for good performance. As you consider your client's performance problems, refer to this checklist to spark your imagination to look at both financial and nonfinancial rewards. Remember that rewards have to be flexible enough to appeal to individual needs; one size doesn't always fit all.

FINANCIAL REWARDS

- ❏ Team-based pay
- ❏ Competency-based pay
- ❏ Profit sharing
- ❏ Knowledge-based pay
- ❏ Corporate stock
- ❏ Bonus

NONFINANCIAL REWARDS

- ❏ Trips
- ❏ Time off
- ❏ Parties
- ❏ High-visibility lunches
- ❏ Club memberships
- ❏ First-class travel
- ❏ Recognition ceremonies: plaques and mementos
- ❏ Corporate driver, limo service

2.13 Where to Look for Business Process Problems

Description

This checklist consists of descriptors of common business processes that can be analyzed for performance characteristics

Why This Tool Is Important

The biggest mistake trainers-turned-performance-consultants make is approaching the performance situation with too narrow a point of view. It is understandable and logical for a trainer to look hardest at the individual persons for evidence of performance problems and to identify the solutions as training solutions—that is, the acquisition of more and better skills or knowledge, or the institution of more and better learning programs.

This tool reminds you as a performance consultant to turn a critical and analytical eye to organizational issues that often begin as "process" problems. The analysis efforts of performance consultants must be balanced to include process performance, organizational performance, and individual performance.

Example of How to Use This Tool

One way to use this tool is to turn it into a matrix with the processes down the side and the process measures across the top:

Accessible Accurate Clear Easy-to-Use Efficient Reliable Responsive Timely Valid

A checkmark in any cell that fits the process you are observing helps clarify your analysis and presents you and your client with a better picture of the company's process performance. Continue your analysis by setting numerical standards for the kind of performance that you and your client consider optimal.

	Accessible	Accurate	Clear	Easy-to-Use	Efficient	Reliable
Information sharing						
Information creation						
Generating feedback						
Using feedback						
Informal communication						
etc.						

Where to Look for Business Process Problems

Instructions: Refer to this checklist in the early stages of planning for a performance consulting assignment. Look for evidence of performance gaps between the optimal and the actual in any of these business processes.

- ❏ Information sharing
- ❏ Information creation
- ❏ Generating feedback
- ❏ Using feedback
- ❏ Informal communication
- ❏ Formal communication
- ❏ Protection of intellectual capital
- ❏ Policy generation
- ❏ Planning
- ❏ Assuring quality products
- ❏ Assuring quality services
- ❏ Collaborating
- ❏ Responding to customers
- ❏ Posting job openings
- ❏ Job description/job design

2.14 Checklist for Organizational Performance

Description

This checklist is a set of scales for rating an organization on many kinds of organizational performance criteria.

Why This Tool Is Important

This checklist carries with it a rating scale from 5 to 1, where 5 represents "yes" and 1 represents "no," indicating your assessment of agreement with each statement about organizational performance. This kind of checklist encourages you to make a judgment about each item, thus helping to give your analysis more differentiation and detail.

Like process performance, organizational performance must be a complement to individual performance. This tool is included so that you can be reminded to think broadly *and* deeply about how the organization/company is performing. Expand the checklist to include any other criteria of organizational performance that seem to be important to your consulting situation.

Example of How to Use This Tool

Use this tool to refine your analysis techniques. Early in the performance consulting process, review this checklist to see the range of criteria for good organizational performance. Realize that "organizational" can mean one team, one department, or one company. You'll need to define exactly what organization you are talking about. Use this rating system to practice thinking specifically about *what* the influences are in organizational performance. At this point, stick to description. You'll deal with the *why* later as you diagnose the problems. (See Chapter 6.)

Checklist for Organizational Performance

Instructions: Use this tool to determine which criteria for good organizational performance are being met and which are not being met. Use it as a descriptive place to start thinking about organizational performance. Place a tic mark on the scale line indicating your judgment of the organization's performance on each item.

Yes	**No**	
5 _____	1	Policies are in place on all important matters.
5 _____	1	Policies are well communicated to all who need to live by them.
5 _____	1	Policies are implemented properly.
5 _____	1	Authority is clearly defined.
5 _____	1	Organizational relationships, structures, and functions are clearly defined.
5 _____	1	Supervisory and reporting relationships are clear.
5 _____	1	Strategic directions are known throughout the organization.
5 _____	1	Human resources practices are consistent with strategy and policy.
5 _____	1	Available information is adequate to the organization's tasks.
5 _____	1	The organization's external environment is stable.
5 _____	1	Each organizational unit is solely responsible for its defined work.
5 _____	1	Information systems work.
5 _____	1	Support is adequate.
5 _____	1	Incentives and rewards encourage performance.
5 _____	1	Sanctions and punishments are equitable and timely.
5 _____	1	Flow of work is appropriate and efficient.
5 _____	1	Decisions are made at the right levels.
5 _____	1	Person-to-person relationships are honest and supportive.

2.15 Guidelines for Management Support of Performance Improvement

Description

Guidelines for management support are presented in five categories: communication, control, facilitation, measures, and resources. With these, you can help your prospective client understand the dimensions of performance that form the foundation for exemplary, high-performance management.

Why This Tool Is Important

While many managers and executives understand the importance of performance improvement, many among even these do not understand the dimensions of performance as delineated in Chapters 1 and 2. Many managers still think of performance in the framework of the annual performance evaluation, which they typically initiate at salary review time.

Needless to say, any kind of performance improvement effort, especially one in which an outside performance consultant is brought into an organization, must have the support of upper management. This is especially critical because in carrying out the various steps of providing consulting services, the consultant and internal collaborators (clients and stakeholders) examine the total organization from many points of view. Performance problems often take several tries, much analysis work, and many perspectives to identify; then they take time, collaborative planning and actions, and more organizational assessments and review to devise solutions. In short, a systematic performance improvement effort unmasks an organization. Managers must be ready for this; consultants must be clear what they need from managers. This tool enables you to help your client managers understand that performance improvement through a systematic performance consulting project is bigger than performance evaluation.

Example of How to Use This Tool

Make a copy of this tool to give to your client as you engage in dialogue about management support of performance improvement. One way to use this tool is to ask for your client's opinion of how important each item is, leading you further into dialogue about the culture that supports performance improvement. Another way to use it is to ask your client to personalize each item and rate their company's managers on each item. Still another way is to give it to managers as a self-assessment tool for managers to rate themselves on each item. If you use it this way, you'll need to develop an answer sheet on which each manager can record answers, for example, on a 5- or 7-point scale for each item, with place on the answer sheet for free response in which narrative comments can be made.

Guidelines for Management Support of Performance Improvement

Instructions: Use this tool in discussions with client managers, to help them and you see the big picture of management behavior in support of performance improvement. Use it also to give yourself some ideas about items to investigate further before you design problem-solving interventions.

Communication
1. Ask questions.
2. Listen.
3. Collaborate.
4. Converse; dialogue with others.
5. Give, receive, and use feedback.
6. Network.
7. Develop and show range of emotion.

Control
8. Analyze and eliminate useless procedures, policies, and practices.
9. Seek wide input about what to do and what not to do.
10. Give praise, rewards, and thanks.
11. Give responsibility for work to individuals who do the work.

Facilitation
12. Provide for information sharing.
13. Encourage teaching and learning on the job.
14. Provide many training options.
15. Demonstrate your commitment to group and team efforts.

Measures
16. Align nonfinancial measures with strategic business directions.
17. Articulate the standards and measures for quality products and services.
18. Support benchmarking.
19. Use 360-degree evaluations of key individuals, including managers.

Resources
20. Develop/maintain organizational structures that support high performance.
21. Provide and promote valid, reliable procedures that are current and effective.
22. Staff organizations adequately.
23. Provide safe buildings and supportive environments in which to work.
24. Provide the right equipment and tools.
25. Be generous with time.
26. Invest financially in high performers.
27. Invest time and money in career development for yourself and others.

Human Performance Glossary

The following alphabetic listing presents the most frequently used and discussed performance terms. Definitions are included even for commonly used words because of their special importance in the context of human performance.

Assumption   A statement of information or a belief accepted as truth without proof; dangerous to performance consulting needs analysis, but always prevalent in problem identification tasks.

Brainstorming   A group effort encouraging creative or divergent thinking, featuring acceptance of all ideas and deferred judgment, operating on a belief that a quantity of ideas leads to quality ideas.

Business need   A numerical goal for an operational unit (manufacturing line, sales force, line of business, department, self-managed team); quantified objectives that are necessary for the business to go forward.

Cause   A root of information or behavior that is responsible for a gap in performance.

Communication   Information transfer from one person to another person, characterized by any or all of these modes: written words, verbal (spoken) words, nonverbal actions, and paraverbal sounds and silences.

Competence   Capability to perform successfully in one's job or life activity.

Competency   An on-the-job behavior representing an internal capability of an individual, often the result of accumulated experience, intuition, and the integration of past learnings; i.e., not a trained behavior.

Conflict   Disagreement, clash, or struggle over objectives or goals and the methods, tactics, and strategies to attain them.

Consensus   General agreement of a majority of the group.

Constructivism   A theory of instructional design that knowledge results from the learner's actively building, that is, constructing, meaning through experience.

Core competency   An essential competency or capability that is critical for successful job performance.

Cost-benefit analysis   Consideration of both positive and negative effects of an action or process; determination of the net effects expressed in both numerical and narrative terms.

Customer capital   The value of a company's relationships with its customers; brand loyalty, tolerance of pricing changes; customer service records, etc.

Deductive approach   Working from general information to specific illustrations or examples; reasoning from general to specific.

Development   Learning that is not specifically tied to a particular job; learning that implies growth, enlargement, and a better state; often associated with the goals of training.

Effectiveness   How much an individual's competencies are used at work; effectiveness is generally influenced by capacity, experience, skills, training, and the will to excel.

Empowerment   The flexibility and freedom to work in self-directed ways; implies the enhancement of self-esteem and self-actualization, as well as the removal of obstacles that contribute to a lack of power.

Environment (job environment)   The total surroundings of individuals at work, including the physical, social, and cultural conditions affecting individual and organizational growth and development.

Experiential learning   A learning model in which participants learn by experiencing in the structured training situation the same skills required of the job.

Feedback   Part of the communication loop in which information about an individual's performance is reported back to the individual by management, colleagues, customers, or electronic reporting systems.

Goal   A target or formulation of an achievement for an individual or organization to pursue within a particular time frame and according to measurable standards.

Group dynamics   The social process by which people interact face to face in groups; especially applied to small groups and teams.

Guided discovery   A learning process that moves from the specific to the general, in which the learner is led by examples, illustrations, and inquiring questions to broad understanding.

Hierarchical organization   An organization of persons classified according to authority or rank; generally associated with a command-and-control way of operating.

Human capital   The knowledge, skills, and competencies that reside within individual employees; seen by many as the most valuable business asset in an information economy. A component of intellectual capital.

Inductive approach   Working from specific examples to general understanding based on the commonalities in the examples; a useful approach to problem identification.

Inference   A deduction based on assumptions; a conclusion based on evidence and logical premise; distinguished from "implication," which is a hint or indirect statement.

Instructional design   A systematic approach to structuring learning experiences based on objectives for the learner; made up of five system elements: analysis, design, development, implementation, and evaluation with feedback to the system at any point.

Intellectual capital   The knowledge that is of value to a company; a broad term generally considered to be made up of the three elements of customer capital, human capital, and structural capital.

Intervention   An intentional, designed change effort aimed at solving a particular performance problem.

Job analysis   Study of a specific job including its people-related, data-related, and things-related characteristics; its requirements and standards of performance relevant to these characteristics; its surrounding context of rules and procedures; its relative importance to business goals; and incentives and staffing issues affecting it.

Knowledge   An accumulation or sum of discoveries, inferences, perceptions, truths, principles, information; in business terms, the pooled expertise of all employees available to add value to a company's services and products; affects both the content and process characteristics of corporate life.

Leader   One who has followers; contrasted with "authority" in that a leader does not necessarily have designated authority or rank by virtue of position or hierarchy; fills the role of encourager, facilitator, and helper to those who follow.

Matrix organization   An organization structure featuring one or more types of classification superimposed on each other, resulting in multiple supervisory chains or reporting relationships for individuals. A typical matrix organization is a team organization superimposed on a hierarchical organization.

Mental model   A representation of the whole body of knowledge unique to an individual; enables the individual to perform complex cognitive tasks. Defining mental models is important in analyzing the causes of performance problems and performance successes.

Nonverbal communication   Transfer of information between two persons that is not dependent on words: physical movements, glances, raised eyebrows, clenched fists silences.

Open question   A question that gives the answerer the opportunity to respond in many ways; most often a question focused on a broad topic; useful in encouraging divergent thinking.

Outcome   An end result of setting goals and working towards meeting them; generally a long-term result and often one over which the employee has diminishing control; contrasted with "performance," which has a more immediate connotation.

Output   The immediate and specific result of work; a service or product created by an individual or an organization, tied directly to work processes.

Organizational culture   The set of beliefs, practices, standards of behavior, and values that is shared by employees and stakeholders or members of the organization.

Organization development   A belief that planned change is possible through a system approach to organizational relationships, including team, intragroup, intergroup, and total organization; a reliance on analysis, design and implementation of interventions, of monitoring, and evaluation and feedback as a basis for development of plans for change; a focus on a range of organizational components from the individual to the environment.

GLOSSARY

Participation   Individual contribution to and involvement in the work of an organization, group, or team; acceptance of shared responsibility for one's actions; related to employee "empowerment" and employee involvement in stock ownership, both of which are considered motivators for employee performance.

Performance   Action in accordance with requirements and expectations; purposeful activity using an individual's mental, physical, and emotional capabilities; generally a qualitative measure of how things are done; often contrasted with "productivity," which is a quantitative measure of output over input.

Performance analysis   Identification of what an organization or an individual must do for the goals and objectives of the business to be accomplished; a comparison of requirements to attitudes, skills, knowledge, processes, the work environment; the answer to the descriptive question, what?

Performance appraisal   The periodic evaluation of employees, usually by supervisors but sometimes by peers and networked colleagues in a "360-degree" manner; also called the "performance review" or "performance evaluation."

Performance consulting   A collaborative problem-solving process involving consultant and client, with the aim of enhancing or improving performance in support of business goals.

Performance deficiency   The identified gap between optimal performance and actual performance; the difference between "what should be" and "what is"; the thing to which an intervention is addressed in the name of performance improvement.

Performance enhancement   An individualized approach to improving performance featuring the psychology of self-assurance, self-control, and mastery over personal performance variables; systematized improvement efforts frequently associated with sports psychology and mental preparation for peak performance, often involving visioning and metacognitive skill development, visualization techniques, role play, and rehearsal; more generally, techniques that can be practiced and learned and that improve one's ability to perform specific tasks with increasing skills.

Performance goal   A specific, observable, measurable, and achievable statement of expected employee behavior.

Performance improvement   A systematic process of closing the gaps in human performance, based on performance analysis and the development of appropriate interventions; including evaluation of planned changed, and giving, receiving, and using feedback.

Performance monitoring   A formalized and systematic observation, review, or study of organizational operations or individual behavior to document what is happening; a formative evaluation of work in progress, as contrasted with a summative evaluation at the completion of work.

Performance objective   A highly structured statement of the behavior expected of an individual at the end of demonstration of skill; usually defined as comprised of three distinct parts: the condition(s) under which the skill must be performed, a description of the behavior(s) characteristic of this skill, and the standard(s) by which successful completion is judged.

Performance technology   A systematic representation of and approach to improving human performance; includes at least these components: (1) analysis, design and implementation of improvement techniques, (2) monitoring, and (3) evaluation of results in an integrated system including inputs, outputs, and feedback; includes both the individual and the organizational environment.

Politics (organizational)   Relationships that protect or enhance an individual's status, future, or self-interest; factional methods, tactics, and interactions that influence individual and organizational behavior.

Potential   Possibility; individual or organizational capacities for achievement; likely results if obstacles to performance are removed.

Practice   Adoption of repetitive patterns of behavior aimed at individual or organizational performance improvement; usually based on identified conceptual models, learning theories, or research results; a typical intervention choice of performance consultants.

Proactive   Being in charge of one's thoughts, actions, and emotions; having the initiative to start processes and projects; having the ability to anticipate activities and events and to act to maximize their effectiveness.

Process   A series of actions and behaviors that yield results; both formalized and informal, moving work along toward a predictable end; often contrasted with "content"; important to performance consultants in analysis and diagnosis steps in performance improvement.

Productivity   A number indicating the ratio of output to input; expressed as a fraction with output as the numerator and input as the denominator; calculated for nations, industries, corporations, organizations, and individuals.

Reactive   Responding to actions, events, behavior of others; altering one's behavior in response to the initiative of others; adapting to change rather than leading it.

Reliability   Performance that is consistent over time; the capacity of an instrument or intervention to produce consistent results with repeated use.

Role   Expected behavior of a person in relationship to other persons; a pattern of activities associated with a function or position within a group; contrasted with "job description," which is specifically prescribed in an employer–employee contract.

Self-managed (self-directed) team   A group of employees with various position titles who have authority over the design of their own group work, responsibility for operational plans and results of work, and financial control of and accountability for their own group projects.

Skill   An individual's proficiency, capacity for expert performance, and ability to use the techniques of reasoning, communication, creative thinking, evaluative deliberation, emotional interactions, and psychomotor behavior; of particular relevance to training needs analysis, instructional design, and instruction.

Status   The ranking of an individual within a group; acquired by overt actions of the individual or bestowed on the individual by the group.

Structural capital   The set of structures, routines, information systems, patents, copyrights, common practices, etc. that remain in place in a company when the employees go home; a component of intellectual capital.

GLOSSARY

System   A dynamic entity comprised of interdependent parts, fundamentally characterized by inputs, processes or throughputs, and outputs; parts in interrelationship that work together for the purpose of the whole.

Task   A discrete, meaningful part of doing a job; has a starting point and ending point; can be easily described and is often coded for ease or difficulty; can be easily related to a performance standard and its accomplishment can be measured; task analysis is an important process in training design.

Training   A teaching and learning process carefully designed to result in personal proficiency in certain identified skills; structured job-related learning; often an intervention of choice for performance improvement; contrasted with "learning," which may or may not be structured, and may or may not be job-related.

Transfer   On-the-job use of skills acquired through training; capacity to apply learning to novel work situations or job challenges.

Validity   Capacity of an instrument, measure, or intervention to do what it claims it can do; an indication of integrity, honesty, and truth.

GLOSSARY

Chapter 3

Tina Trainer Tries the Tools

This is the final chapter in Part 1, "Moving from Training to Performance Consulting." In Chapter 3, you'll find a synthesis of all you've learned so far by reading this toolbook, and a presentation of information in the form of six minicase studies of the sort that face trainers in transition to performance consultants.

Each case is stated in terms that are familiar to trainers. Tina's choice of tool(s) to use in dealing with each case is reproduced on the right-hand page. For each case, her options are outlined. Her consultant thinking is suggested, including references to key points in the tool as Tina begins to plan her performance-consulting action steps. Chapter 3 ends with "Final Words of Support for New Performance Consultants," Tool 3.7.

These are the six cases in Chapter 3:

- *Patient charts.* Sloppy and inconsistent reporting of patient data on Floor 2 patient charts.

- *Knowledge resource base.* Poor participation of technical managers in the new knowledge resource base.

- *Management budget.* Unrealistic budget; all operations heads are overbudget.

- *Sales.* Market is stolen by competitor; sales are falling.

- *Chinese guests.* Engineering customers are due to return home to China in five days. What can we do to maximize our time with them?

- *Teamwork.* Teamwork has degenerated into business-as-usual after six months of trying to be a team.

Tina Trainer's Case Study on Patient Charts

The Quality Manager of a regional hospital did a study of how data were being entered by health care professionals on in-patients' charts. He discovered that the charts of the second floor (medical) patients were particularly sloppy and inconsistent. He asked Tina to train all second-floor physicians, physician assistants, nurses, LPNs, and aides in how to write sentences and in the importance of accurate and useful completion of the patient chart.

Tina's Options

1. Develop a course in response to the Quality Manager's request.

2. Make copies of the section on patient charts in the Policy and Procedures manual, send it with a strongly worded cover memo suggesting that each person on the "hit list" study the patient chart information and shape up. Hire a local community college English teacher to run a workshop in the hospital for the second-floor personnel.

3. Make a videotape using second-floor personnel as actors—maybe a physician, physician assistant, nurse, LPN, aide—to demonstrate the correct way to complete a patient chart. Send it around the staff so that each can study it, and hope that they can copy the correct procedures when they have to do a patient chart the next time.

4. Don't do anything until you ask a few questions, like, "Why only the second floor charts?" "Is one type of care provider worse than another in terms of performance?" "Is the problem really that they can't write a straight sentence?"

Tina's Consultant Thinking

I really have to hold myself back from continuing to think in terms only of training solutions (options 1, 2, 3). I should take another look at Tool 1.3, Worksheet on Thinking Styles: Convergent versus Divergent Thinking. I have good intuition about why there might be problems on the second floor (item 7), and I think I have a grasp of the big picture around here (item 11). For one thing, the second floor is a medical floor where patients are more ill with longer-term problems than patients on other floors. The new administrator has been working with second-floor staff particularly in the past few months to develop a culture of caring and the human touch. She encourages more frequent visits to patients by a variety of staff. Perhaps staff are misinterpreting this new friendliness as a change away from the data-intensive business approach that we've had for years. She and the Quality Manager seem to come from different planets. It seems to me that they need to get their act together before we beat up on the second-floor staff. Training is not the place to start. I need to check out my assumptions first.

Tina's Choice for Case Study on Patient Charts

1.3 Worksheet on Thinking Styles: Convergent versus Divergent Thinking

Instructions: Use this worksheet to rate your natural tendency to think in a particular way. Simply place a mark on the line after each statement indicating your self-rating of the item. Use a 4-point scale, where 1 = never and 4 = always; a mark anywhere on the line is acceptable. There are no right or wrong responses; use the results of your work to make plans to develop your capacity for divergent thinking if your patterns are overwhelmingly convergent. This worksheet is appropriate for use in team training.

Convergent Thinking

1. I like to follow directions.
2. I feel best when "loops" are closed.
3. I plan carefully to finish lessons.
4. I prefer concrete to abstract.
5. I like to take things to logical conclusions.
6. I need everything in order before I begin.

Divergent Thinking

7. I work best from my own intuition.
8. I thrive on variety.
9. I like to generate options.
10. I prefer synthesis over analysis.
11. "Big pictures" fascinate me.
12. Freedom is more important to me than discipline.

1 = Never	2 = Sometimes	3 = Often	4 = Always

Plans for developing divergent thinking:

What?

- When?
- With Whom?
- Why?

95

Tina Trainer's Case Study on the Knowledge Resource Base

In a corporatewide effort to become a learning company, we have established a Knowledge Resource Base (KRB) of information about unique ways to solve production and service problems. Management expects each employee above a certain salary level and position grade to contribute regularly to this database so that information can be shared widely. We've noticed that 80 percent of our highest-level technical managers contribute very little of substance or contribute nothing at all. There have been complaints about this from those who do contribute regularly, along with a request for the training department to do something about it. Tina Trainer is assigned the task of following up on the situation.

Tina's Options

1. Find out names of the 80 percent; look at their reporting relationships.

2. See if they joined the company after the big rollout of KRB, and need training in what's expected of them as well as how to use it for their own knowledge building.

3. Ask those who do contribute regularly what they think the problem is.

Tina's Consultant Thinking

What a revelation: Nearly all of the 80 percent are persons for whom English is their second language. When I talked with a sample of regular contributors, I discovered also that they complained about the target group's poor presentation skills and poor written skills. Formal show-and-tell sessions and formal memos were painful. I also discovered that the majority of the 80 percent group were Asian and Latin American, where cultural norms generally influence behavior in the direction of never asking for help and never admitting that you don't know something. They know what's expected of them, and they know how to use the system. They also are extremely afraid of looking foolish in front of their colleagues. They would rather risk complaints about nonparticipation than contribute poorly developed ideas in less than perfect English. They have a training problem, but it's not the one we first thought it might be. It's not an attitude problem; it's lack of skills and guided practice in using the English language. As a trainer, I know a skills gap when I see one. As a consultant, I am not afraid to suggest a training solution after I've examined the problem's environment—in this case the cultural environment.

Tina's Choice for Case Study on The Knowledge Resource Base

1.11 Where To Look for Support as You Move toward Performance Consulting

Instructions: Check as many sources as apply to your situation. Add others as appropriate.

Notes

____ 1. Informal internal change agents (individuals)

____ 2. Lists of competencies from professional associations

____ 3. Evaluations of past consultants

____ 4. Past consultants' end-of-project reports

____ 5. Policies

____ 6. Procedures manuals

____ 7. Performance reviews (your own and others)

____ 8. Corporate annual reports

____ 9. Corporate goals, vision, and mission statements

____ 10. Three-year stock performance history and trends

____ 11. Current business books

____ 12. Professional journals

____ 13. College courses

____ 14. _____

____ 15. _____

____ 16. _____

1.15 How to Establish Credibility as a Consultant

Instructions: Use this checklist each time you decide to seek a consulting contract.

____ 1. Demonstrate your own competent performance, past or present.

____ 2. Prove that you are a continuous learner.

____ 3. Use your network of personal professional connections.

____ 4. Demonstrate solid content information.

____ 5. Be able to choose and use a wide variety of process interventions.

____ 6. Know yourself: your own needs and wants from consulting, be able to articulate your values, know your preferred working styles

____ 7. Accept responsibility.

____ 8. Be fiscally accountable.

____ 9. Provide complete, accurate, relevant, necessary and sufficient information.

____ 10. Act with integrity.

Tina Trainer's Case Study on the Management Budget

A large church organization was in trouble with its budget. Heads of programs and operational managers for several years seemed to budget on vision rather than on reality. The new Executive Director decided to get the management budgeting process under control, and called Tina Trainer to act as an external performance consultant to the management group. She eagerly initiated discussions with the Executive Director prior to developing a consulting proposal.

Tina's Options

1. Assume that "visionary" is the role that church administrative types instinctively adopt and prefer; assume also, therefore, that reality-based budgeting needs to be taught to these managers.

2. Suggest to the Executive Director that several levels of budget workshops should be designed and delivered to the group. Suggest that the organization's treasurer and office assistants be invited to the workshops too.

3. Step back from these assumptions and think about other possible influences on the budgeting process that are not related to a lack of information or knowledge of the budget process. Don't be too quick to engage the Executive Director in discussions of workshops. Investigate first to frame the right questions on financial health.

Tina's Consultant Thinking

I'm glad I remembered Tool 2.3, Variables to Watch Out for in a Consulting Assignment *before I got too far along the path to workshops. I am drawn to checklist items 4, 5, 6, 8, and 10. I'd like to investigate the vision approach relative to these items on incentives, rewards, and punishment. I have a feeling that "visionary" could be a convenient role behind which to hide; reality-based budgeting is too painful because the money just isn't coming in the way it used to a decade ago. As long as the endowments spin off growth funds, the organization has the luxury of covering shortfalls in reality-based programs and operations—that is, the luxury of being guided by vision rather than being grounded in reality. I'd like to find out the expectations of the governing board, the kinds of numbers rewarded by acclamation or otherwise, the incentives around the office for "visionary" thinking, the personal and organizational motivations to discourage reality-based budgeting, and the punishments directed at either budgeting approach. I believe that this is a case in which the definition of the performance gap is going to be found in something related to motivation and incentives. These are smart people; they know how to do a budget. They probably don't need workshops.*

Tina's Choice for Case Study on the Management Budget

2.3 Variables to Watch Out for in a Consulting Assignment

Instructions: Use this as a checklist of variables that apply to your own particular consulting situation. Review the list item by item before you scope out your project and before you meet with a client. Use it to review the possibilities in performance consulting so that you remember to think of all contingencies as you approach the design of a consulting job.

- [ ] 1. Current performance
- [ ] 2. Desired performance
- [ ] 3. Definition of the gap in performance
- [ ] 4. Motivation
- [ ] 5. Incentives
- [ ] 6. Rewards
- [ ] 7. Objectives
- [ ] 8. Expectations
- [ ] 9. Bias
- [ ] 10. Punishment
- [ ] 11. Feedback
- [ ] 12. Intellectual competencies
- [ ] 13. Physical competencies
- [ ] 14. Emotional competencies
- [ ] 15. Job skills
- [ ] 16. Job knowledge
- [ ] 17. Data
- [ ] 18. Information
- [ ] 19. Time
- [ ] 20. Financial resources/support
- [ ] 21. Procedures
- [ ] 22. Pay
- [ ] 23. Benefits
- [ ] 24. Tools and equipment
- [ ] 25. Work environment
- [ ] 26. Training/career development
- [ ] 27. Supervision
- [ ] 28. Management
- [ ] 29. Staffing
- [ ] 30. Business goals

Tina Trainer's Case Study on Sales

Sales of computers had fallen dramatically. In recent months, three new competing manufacturing companies had opened—offering low prices, come-on promotions, big advertising spending, and motivated sales forces—and the market was shattered. Tina is under the gun to find the hottest sales training consultant fast to get the sales force in tune with the latest sales techniques and maybe shed some light on what the competition is doing that we're not.

Tina's Options

1. Pay big bucks to get the best name in the business ASAP. Train within the month.

2. Do a benchmark study on at least four companies with a reputation for superior sales teams. Develop internal training based on what we find during benchmarking.

   Hire contract instructional designers to help. Promise training within three months.

3. Interview each sales person to get a feel for the range of selling expertise represented by our team; identify the experts and set up a formal coaching program for them to share their expertise with the less-than-expert individuals.

4. Look around the company for organizations and influences that have an impact or relationship to sales. Figure out if something other than sales training is needed.

Tina's Consultant Thinking

This could be an organizational problem, not a knowledge and skills problem. Why do I keep driving myself crazy thinking like a trainer? If I implemented either option 1 or option 2, I'd be wasting a pile of money and precious time on training that didn't address the problem, because I hadn't defined the problem. I would be blindly accepting someone else's definition of the problem. Option 3 sounds like a good idea, but it too is a training solution. Option 4 is a performance consultant's approach. It doesn't feel as familiar and comfortable as training approaches, but Tools 2.16 and 2.9 help to put it into context. I notice that an item about "adequate support" appears on both the individual tool and the organizational tool. This leads me to want to look closely at our hotline/helpline service. We've had some complaints in the past about not being able to get through to the service. My hunch is that customers and potential customers turn to our competitors because they can't get through to us. I'll make a few phone calls to competitors' help lines to test my hunch. Maybe helplines is where we should do a quick and dirty benchmarking study; maybe activating another hotline/helpline and changing our message to include a soft sales pitch during help calls would be a good idea. We could do this within a week.

Tina's Choice for Case Study on Sales

2.9 Causes of Poor Performance

Instructions: Review this list as you begin to diagnose human performance problems. This list can be especially useful as you prepare to analyze performance needs. Use this list in conjunction with the three other lists, Tools 2.6, 2.7, and 2.8.

___ Unattainable objectives

___ Wide gaps between actual and optimal performance

___ Inadequate training

___ Inadequate resources

___ Lack of support

___ Broken or outdated equipment

___ Lack of knowledge and skills

___ Bad timing

___ Anger, fear, depression, out-of-control emotions

___ Inflexibility

___ Lack of self-regulation ability

___ Unethical behavior

___ Unsafe or hostile work environment

___ Unclear business goals

2.14 Checklist for Organizational Performance

Instructions: Use this tool to determine which criteria for good organizational performance are being met and which are not being met. Use it as a descriptive place to start thinking about organizational performance. Place a tic mark on the scale line indicating your judgment of the organization's performance on each item.

Yes   **No**

5 _____ 1   Policies are in place on all important matters.

5 _____ 1   Policies are well communicated to all who need to live by them.

5 _____ 1   Policies are implemented properly.

5 _____ 1   Authority is clearly defined.

5 _____ 1   Organizational relationships, structures, and functions are clearly defined.

5 _____ 1   Supervisory and reporting relationships are clear.

5 _____ 1   Strategic directions are known throughout the organization.

5 _____ 1   Human resources practices are consistent with strategy and policy.

5 _____ 1   Available information is adequate to the organization's tasks.

5 _____ 1   The organization's external environment is stable.

5 _____ 1   Each organizational unit is solely and unambiguously responsible for its defined work.

5 _____ 1   Information systems work.

5 _____ 1   Support is adequate.

5 _____ 1   Incentives and rewards encourage performance.

5 _____ 1   Sanctions and punishments are equitable and timely.

5 _____ 1   Flow of work is appropriate and efficient.

5 _____ 1   Decisions are made at the right levels.

5 _____ 1   Person-to-person relationships are honest and supportive.

Tina Trainer's Case Study on Chinese Guests

A leadership team of 12 managers of engineering and software departments and their lead technicians have been in residence at our company for two weeks, guests of our management. They were the key players in a multimillion-dollar deal in which our intellectual property, in the form of simulation software programs, is being licensed by their company. Our expertise will be transferred to two of their chemical processing plants in China. All contracts have been signed during these two weeks, and the Chinese guests are due to return to China at the end of next week. Tina Trainer has been asked by the Vice President of Human Resources, her boss, to keep them busy for five days.

Tina's Options

1. Schedule them to sit in on our next week's classes for new software developers.

2. Make a goodie bag of catalogs, course manuals, overheads, and other training department materials for each person to take home.

3. Quickly put together two or three days of role-playing workshops around a focus group format, so that they can orient their thinking toward applications. Use our best facilitator and a simple one- or two- page agenda (to save preparation time).

4. Check with the Vice President of Sales and Director of Engineering to see what they think would be the most useful things our guests could learn in five days.

5. Ask the guests what they want to learn in the next five days.

Tina's Consultant Thinking

Well, for sure, the easiest option is option 1. But that's risky because I know most of our guests are very experienced software developers, and this particular week of classes will be at an elementary level. That could backfire. They'd like option 2, but, again, we'd risk giving them irrelevant information—nice to know, but not need to know. Option 3 might be fun, and we could do it. It would be more targeted, more personalized than the other options. Maybe we could even involve our sales and engineering staff. Obviously, we should begin with option 5, and flesh out what we learn from our guests themselves with intelligence from our VP of Sales and Director of Engineering. This is a case in which 20 individuals need to have a performance gap identified and closed—where are they now versus where would they like to be at the end of next week? The issues are realism and utility. We have five days. What can we do that will be most useful to our guests in this timeframe? The company's credibility is definitely on the line at this euphoric time of having just gotten a major contract. I cannot let invalid training "solutions" destroy our good name and potential future in China. Plus, we shouldn't give away the store. Who knows—they might want to buy training at a later time. Save training solutions for training problems. Tool 2.10 can help me think through my approach.

Tina's Choice for Case Study on Chinese Guests

2.10 How to Determine What Is versus What Should Be

Instructions: Use this checklist as a design tool to help you determine an approach to analyzing the gap in performance, that is, what is versus what should be. (Detailed steps follow in Chapters 5 and 6.) Use this checklist to first expand and then to focus your thinking about gap analysis.

— 1. Distinguish between wants and needs.

— 2. Consider organizational, team, and individual needs.

— 3. State clearly the desired performance (what should be).

— 4. State clearly the actual performance (what is).

— 5. Match up what the client says the problem is and what you see as the performance gap; compare, contrast, break into subproblems.

— 6. Decide where you can correlate the defined gaps with stated company goals, mission, business plans.

— 7. Guard against being simply reactive to the client's statements.

— 8. Make no assumptions and accept no assumptions that training is the answer to performance needs or the way to close the gaps.

— 9. Guard against acceptance of national surveys or journalistic opinions as valid input to your analysis of gaps; design your own gap-identifying data collection instruments and processes.

— 10. Look for consequences and causes in the internal capacities of individuals and in the work environment that surrounds individuals.

— 11. Look for gaps due to data, resources, motivation, knowledge and skill, and physical, intellectual, and emotional capacity.

— 12. Be proactive in questioning, in listening, in communicating, in designing, and in planning; identify gaps early in your consulting assignment.

— 13. Don't ignore the gap assessment; take the time to do this process carefully.

Tina Trainer's Case Study on Teamwork

The team is falling apart. After six months of trying, they've lapsed back into business as usual—protect what you know, cover all the bases, live and let live, do only the work you get reviewed on, etc. Tina Trainer is called in to negotiate with the team leader about developing a seminar on group dynamics and communication. The company says it is committed to teams.

Tina's Options

1. Show the team leader the course catalog and let her choose which communications courses she wants; steer her in the direction of the courses in which group process is a strong component.

2. Offer to find off-the-shelf courses from reputable training suppliers; suggest that they might be less expensive than developing a customized in-house seminar.

3. Forget training negotiation for now; focus instead on performance needs of individual team members.

Tina's Consultant Thinking

Maybe I am finally getting it right! After writing down options 1 and 2, I see that both are built on the assumption that the team's problem is a lack of knowledge or skills, that is, a training problem. Of course, I know that performance is broader than training and that teamwork is a complex business process that's far bigger than knowledge and skills. In the big picture, six months is not a long time in which to expect changed behaviors to be institutionalized. On the other hand, six months is a reasonable amount of time in which to have accumulated evidence of types of problems and a considerable range of experience in dealing with them. Tool 2.11, Chart of Competencies, shows clearly that competency is what we need to be talking about, not necessarily skills and knowledge. I am especially drawn to the intellectual competencies of "can learn from mistakes" and "decision making." We need to talk with team members about the environment around here regarding both these areas of competence. I'm also drawn to the emotional competencies of "assertiveness" and "has a range of emotions." It seems to me that for years employees have not been encouraged to be assertive, nor have they been supported in developing their emotional selves. I think that there are corporate culture issues here that need sorting out before we negotiate for new training.

Tina's Choice for Case Study on Teamwork

2.11 Chart of Competencies

Instructions: Use this chart to analyze the totality of the worker's capacity to perform. Add or delete items to customize the chart to your situation.

PHYSICAL

— Speed and accuracy of response to stimulus

— Reliability of spatial orientation   — Timing

— Strength   — Consistency

— Muscle flexibility   — Neatness

— General health   — _____

— Reliability of pattern repetition   — _____

     — _____

INTELLECTUAL

— Knowledge of job content

— Oral communication   — Synthesis

— Written communication   — Evaluation

— Can learn from mistakes   — Organization

— Decision making   — Planning

— Analysis   — Logic, mathematics

     — _____

EMOTIONAL

— Assertiveness

— Sense of self   — Enthusiasm

— Self-confidence   — Kindness

— Pride in work   — Respect

— Can deal with ambiguity   — Generosity, sharing

— Has a long fuse   — _____

— Has a range of emotions   — _____

     — _____

VALUES AND BELIEFS

— Loyal

— Moral   — Objective

— Unbiased   — Accepts responsibility

— Principled   — Courageous

— Follows rules   — Honest

— Independent   — Trustworthy

     — _____

Final Words of Support for New Performance Consultants

Don't regret becoming a trainer. Trainers are generally lovable types, warm and friendly, bright and dedicated, and often the ones weary managers turn to to have their problems solved. The trouble is that the problems are not always training problems, and the training solution is wrong for the individual and for the organization. What seems like the right approach—that is, training is good for you—turns out to be wrong, expensive, time-consuming, unaccountable, unmeasurable, and unproductive.

So, here's the last word to those who find it hard getting unstuck from the habit of "thinking training." These strategies are personally useful as you gain confidence to venture out of the field of training. They are especially useful as a framework for discussion with a client who also might find it hard getting unstuck from always seeing training as the solution. Your actions and dialogue with clients should reflect these strategies and involve the clients in them:

1. Stop and think before you choose a training solution.

2. Take care to define the problem before you define solution options.

3. Don't waste people's time and money.

4. Be assertive; have confidence in your intuitions and your investigations.

5. Be proactive; caution against automatic reactive thought and action.

6. Network, cultivate relationships out of your normal range of associates, collaborate, and seek input from a variety of sources.

7. Develop your own set of information-seeking skills; expand your ability to target sources and to find information that you need. Strengthen your computer skills, and your skills at making sense of financial, engineering, and sales data.

8. Learn to talk business. Learn as much as you can about your client company's customers, organizational structure, vision of itself, plans or talk about its intellectual capital, and reputation among its competitors.

9. Relate whatever you do to the client company's business goals.

A Ten-Step Guide to the Performance Consulting Process

Four chapters make up Part II, "A Ten-Step Guide to the Performance Consulting Process." Containing ten steps in performance consulting, these chapters are: "Contracting," "Analyzing Performance," "Diagnosing Performance Problems," and "Designing Performance Solutions." Altogether, 35 tools are provided in Part II to help you do your job as a performance consultant. These tools zero in on the most important tasks of performance consulting, in the sequence you would normally perform them. Unlike Part I, which helps trainers broaden their perspective and develop a performance consulting mindset, Part II deals with the specifics of doing performance consulting.

The format for tools in Part II is slightly different from that in Part I. Left-hand pages in this part feature a section called "What You Already Know That Can Help You." This narrative section of each tool helps you remember to bring forward into your work as a performance consultant many specific skills and intuitions you've gained as a trainer—both explicit and tacit knowledge. This section shows you how to adapt and transfer what you've learned and done as a trainer to your new role as performance consultant. This feature is meant to boost your self-confidence with helpful hints, new awareness, and useful applications as you begin performance consulting or continue to refine your set of performance consulting skills. Left-hand pages in Part II also feature a section of explanation that is more extensive and goes a little deeper than the descriptions in Part I.

Each step in the performance consulting process is introduced in one of the following four chapters. Each step is succinctly explained before the tools for its implementation are presented.

Chapter 4

Contracting

Step 1: Get a good contract.

This is the first of four chapters containing 10 key steps in performance consulting. This chapter is especially important because it details the issues in contracting, perhaps the most difficult of all steps for trainers to understand. Chapter 4 contains twelve tools just on the techniques of getting a good contract. This chapter sets the standard for the next three chapters. Like Chapters 1 and 2, a right-hand page provides the tool itself, and a left-hand page provides narrative commentary about the tool and the problems it helps you solve.

Tools in Chapter 4

STEP 1

Step 1: Get a good contract.
This means getting what you want
and need in the contract
and
giving the client
what the client wants and needs.
Tools in this chapter help you
Negotiate and write a good contract.

4.1 Where to Go for Good Data before Contracting

Description

This checklist is a reminder of where to go for useful data before you write the contract.

Explanation

Use this precontract data collection as a way to educate yourself about the business, the company, and the particular man or woman who is likely to be your client. The first four sources in the checklist are self-explanatory. However, the last item in the checklist, "Your Client," needs elaboration. Try to get your client (prospective client) to take a few minutes to make some lists for you. Tell him/her that you expect this to be a collaborative relationship for the duration of the time you spend together and that the contracting process will go more smoothly if you know "hot buttons" now. Suggest at this early stage that you need to know these things to write a valid and useful contract. Emphasize that the client needs to be honest with you before you enter into contract negotiations so that you both understand the full dimensions of the proposed work. Remind the client that a contract is a 50/50 deal, that you'll do your best to generate a good contract that satisfies the client's needs, wants, and concerns, and that a little help from the client up front can make it a lot easier to do so.

What You Already Know That Can Help You

Trainers who've been around corporate classrooms for awhile no doubt have come to appreciate the value of *continuous learning*. You've probably run programs around "quality improvement" or "the learning organization" that have preached this message. You might even see these words on your company's corporate mission statement or in your own training department's strategic plan or statement of values. If you haven't adopted continuous learning as one of your own personal values, you're at least aware of its importance from so much corporate exposure in recent years around training rooms.

This tool helps you to become a continuous learner. It is a reminder that you need to get your antennae up and sense your client's environment. You need tools like this one early in the contracting process to encourage yourself to think broadly as you gather data.

Where to Go for Good Data before Contracting

Instructions: These sources can be helpful pointers to you as you anticipate a more extensive search later for adequate and valid data of both the objective sort and the personal sort.

Collect precontract data to provide yourself with "talking points" during contract negotiations with the client. Be informed about and interested in the company and the industry you'll be working in. It is always tempting to focus only on clients and their personalities at contract time; go one step further and be informed about the business you'll be a part of. Allow yourself enough time (several weeks) to search for, find, and assimilate the data you think you'll need for successful contracting. Remember, at this point you have no formal relationship with the company; you have no right to be a nuisance. Ask for information that is public information.

Here's where to look:

- *Public information/public relations office:* Annual reports, corporate mission and vision statements, names of directors and top executives, copies of company newsletters, research reports, and magazines.

- *Sales office:* Product line information, client lists, industry watch reports.

- *Newspapers:* Articles about the company, articles about the company's competitors, features on company employees, editorials and letters to the editor referencing the company.

- *Public library or Internet:* National business reports rating the company on a variety of standards and practices. Ask the reference librarian for help; community college libraries are great resources.

- *Your client:* Lists of the client's needs and wants, risks and concerns; a list of persons your client believes have a stake in the outcome of this project; a list of specific products (reports, formulae, other documents) the client expects; a list of deadlines that are critical to the client; a current organization chart indicating reporting relationships.

4.2 Checklist for Initiative and Assertiveness in Contracting

Description

This checklist helps you to get your half of the deal.

Explanation

Words in parentheses explain how to address specific contracting points in a way that's fair to both yourself and to the client.

_____ 1. Specific project objectives *(It's what you see, not necessarily what they say; be specific but within a broader organizational context, giving yourself some flexibility.)*

_____ 2. Clear parameters of analysis *(Be clear about where you will not look.)*

_____ 3. Description of kinds of and probable sources of information that you need and will seek *(Be specific; give them fair warning; stand your ground here.)*

_____ 4. Space and materials support you need *(Be fair; absorb some of these costs yourself, but specify exactly what you expect them to provide—e.g., office, phone, copying, computer, training on their systems, etc.)*

_____ 5. Exactly whom you expect to work with from the client organization(s) *(Name names; if you don't know names, name organizations and specify that you want an official representative from that group.)*

_____ 6. Your expectations regarding project communication and in-process reports, including in-process feedback from the client to you *(Write into the contract a periodic, regular status report, e.g., every two weeks; specify its format, to whom and in what setting it will be delivered; go for a face-to-face meeting so that you get some feedback from the client too on a regular, expected, basis; avoid surprises in communication and feedback.)*

_____ 7. Confidentiality and protection of intellectual property agreements *(Insist that your investigations and work remain confidential and that they will protect what you share with them; likewise, give them assurance you will do the same for them and their materials.)*

_____ 8. Project deliverables *(Be specific: e.g., 300-page competitive analysis report; a new system for order-entry, pilot-tested by August 10, etc.)*

_____ 9. Timeline *(Sometimes it helps you to do two timelines, one general and one specific; perhaps write into the contract a midproject timeline review.)*

_____ 10. Your consultant role in the project *(Are you an expert, pair of hands, collaborator?)*

What You Already Know That Can Help You

The most important thing in using this checklist is to develop an attitude first—an attitude of assertiveness. Trainers recognize this issue of assertiveness and initiative if you've been involved with teaching *empowerment* workshops, *diversity management* seminars, *sales training*, workshops on *personality type* and *learning styles*, and workshops for clerical workers who want to *move into management*. Use the ideas you're familiar with in these training settings to remind yourself to be assertive in your contracting with a client. Don't try to please; try to be fair.

Checklist for Initiative and Assertiveness in Contracting

Instructions: Review this checklist item by item before you finalize writing the contract. Be sure that you have written into the contract the working arrangements and support that you consider your fair share of the deal.

____ 1. Specific project objectives

____ 2. Clear parameters of analysis

____ 3. Description of kinds of and probable sources of information that you need and will seek

____ 4. Space and materials support you need

____ 5. Exactly whom you expect to work with from the client organization(s)

____ 6. Your expectations regarding project communication and in-process reports, including in-process feedback from the client to you

____ 7. Confidentiality and protection of intellectual property agreements

____ 8. Project deliverables

____ 9. Timeline

____ 10. Your consultant role in the project

This list is loosely based on the work of Peter Block, 1981, p. 52.

4.3 Techniques for Negotiation and Selling in the Contract

Description

This is a list of techniques used by consultants to negotiate the contract fairly to both parties and to sell their services.

Explanation

This checklist contains important processes that are useful in negotiation. Key-words in the various items are related to communication skills, skills of analysis and being specific, and emotional skills of showing consideration and ensuring fairness. Review the list before meeting with your client for negotiation of the contract. Operate from strength on each of these items; before you meet the client for a contracting session, get more help for yourself in any area in which you feel you are not strong. This checklist breaks down the negotiation process into skill areas, making it easier for you to pursue a plan for self-improvement if that's what you need.

What You Already Know That Can Help You

Instructional designers and instructors pay attention to *content* and *process* as they create and deliver training. The techniques listed here also pay attention to both content and process, spelling out how various communication processes can give you the upper hand in negotiation and what specifics of content you'll want to include. To carry out effective contract negotiation, you need to pay equal attention to content and to process, as you did in training development and delivery, as you go after a good contract.

Techniques for Negotiation and Selling in the Contract

Instructions: Refer to this list before entering into the contracting process.

1. Articulate your needs—personal and professional—to the client. Don't be shy. Remember that you are a party to the contract too.

2. Likewise, be sure that you also encourage clients to articulate their needs—personal and professional.

3. Have a dialogue with the client to resolve any differences in articulated project needs. Insist on an equal playing field; that is, if you intend to bring along members of your consulting staff, invite clients to bring along an equal number of their staff.

4. Sharpen your questioning skills before meeting with the client. Asking good questions is far more important than giving "answers" at the contracting stage.

5. Do your homework prior to the contracting session. Know what the client's business is all about—cities in which there are branches or factories, trends over the past few years regarding stock performance, the corporate mission statement, who the CEO and Board Chairman are, the names of major product lines, the company's competitors, etc. Be prepared to initiate discussion about the larger business picture.

6. Probe to clarify and verify issues of client control, mutual accountability, political danger zones, and any other internal "land mines" that might be buried. Aim to bring all out in the open so that both contracting parties understand and agree on the problem issues. Don't exclude this step: You'll get in trouble later if you do. Take the time and energy up front to expose all secrets.

7. Be specific about the deliverables of the project and write them into the contract.

8. Be assertive about your own ability to work with the client to identify and solve problems. Negotiate from the strength of necessary and sufficient information and a good measure of confidence in the client and in yourself.

9. Show genuine appreciation to the client for the demonstrated faith in you. Thank the client for inviting you to participate in this process of negotiation.

10. Assure the client that you will respect your position of access and the client's vulnerability while you are working together with the client on this project.

4.4 Kinds of Data to Avoid in Contracting

Description

This is a checklist of kinds of data to avoid in contracting.

Explanation

A consultant is not part of a company's staff, and the freedom and responsibility that accompany this fact are key reasons why consultants are in business. Keep reminding yourself that you work *for* yourself, *with* others. That is, you don't work for "XYZ" company or even for "Mr. Q." Such reminders can help you to stay focused on your tasks and your project. Guard against trying to wiggle yourself into the company grapevines, watercooler networks, copy machine clubs, and Friday night happy hours. Be careful where you look for data and what things influence you to turn data into information. This tool can help you avoid some traps.

"Necessary and sufficient" is the rule. Learn to focus on what you understand as the intent of the consulting arrangement. Go for quality of data, not necessarily quantity. A focused contract is your goal; be careful to not go astray early in the data collection. It's much easier to negotiate additional specific contracts later than to write and be held to a fuzzy contract now. Let the data collection help you, not mire you in extraneous and irrelevant verbiage.

What You Already Know That Can Help You

As an employee yourself you know what gets people in trouble. Trouble means wasted time, hurt feelings, causing anger in others, becoming angry yourself, shooting from the hip, mouthing off, acting from impulse or bias, losing focus, compromising quality, smoke and mirrors, and a host of other workplace behaviors that Scot Adams and Dilbert—even Dogbert—love to uncover and expose. As a consultant, you need especially to avoid getting trapped in the data originating from these unfavorable situations. As a trainer, you have been sensitized to *standards of workplace equal opportunity*. You certainly know what to avoid if you've ever taught courses or workshops in affirmative action or sexual harassment, valuing diversity, and employee empowerment. Use the "things to avoid" parts of these workshops to give yourself a foundation for thinking about kinds of data to avoid when entering a consulting agreement. Practice the art of "transfer of training" on yourself.

Kinds of Data to Avoid in Contracting

Instructions: Read this before you ask for data from the client or from other sources prior to contracting. Before you write the contract, also review the checklist. Check off each item as you assure yourself that you have avoided each one.

Avoid these kinds of data:

___ 1. Rumor and hearsay

___ 2. General targets

___ 3. Unspecified sources

___ 4. Unclear timeframes

___ 5. Obtuse or convoluted language

___ 6. Statistics that are irrelevant to this project

___ 7. Evaluative opinion (concentrate instead on description)

___ 8. Stereotypes and bias

___ 9. Ammunition for attack

4.5 How to Identify Stakeholders

Description

This is a list of where to look for clients and other key players in the client network of influence.

Explanation

Stakeholders are persons who have an investment in your work. They can have many points of view:

- Their jobs depend on your findings or recommendations.

- They are responsible for budget or other financial implications of your findings or recommendations.

- They have operational responsibility for fixing a problem you might identify.

- They will benefit in either status or pay from your work.

- They are in charge of the quality of the work environment that forms your working environment during the consulting engagement.

- Their production or sales quotas will be affected by what you find or recommend. They report to your client or your client reports to them.

- They simply care.

Stakeholders can be identified by using a web or organizational mapping device. First identify your client (not necessarily the person who is your "contact"). Then connect your client to any others throughout the company, including suppliers and key customers, who have a stake in the outcome of your work. Here's an example:

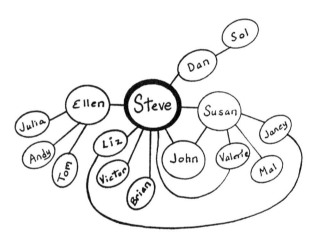

What You Already Know That Can Help You

Trainers who have participated in *needs assessments* or *front-end analyses* understand the concept of stakeholders. Instructional designers and training managers who have followed the *Instructional System Design (ISD)* principles in the development of training also relate to the importance of identifying and meeting the needs—emotional needs and content needs—of persons with a stake in the outcome of training or in this case of performance consulting. In training needs assessment, stake-holders include trainees' managers or customers, certifying boards such as OSHA or unions, affirmative action or EEO officers, hiring personnel, the trainer's supervisor.

The process of identification is similar, but performance consulting looks more widely, that is, beyond training.

How to Identify Stakeholders

Instructions: Refer to this list before you write the contract so that you allow the time, resources, and strategy for dealing with all stakeholders. Turn your list into a map or a web if that helps you see the relationships.

Stakeholders

The **client**—
probably a manager or person with operations responsibility

The **contact(s)**—
persons provided to you, generally to handle the scheduling and paperwork

The **boss**—
the person to whom the client reports

Direct reports—
persons who report to your client

Cross-functional support persons—
persons who cross-function (human resources and personnel specialists, trainers, quality specialists, safety specialists, maintenance staff, legal staff, accountants, information technologists, teams) with tangential interest in your client's organization

Sales persons—
who need to know what's new in the company—and what's on its way out

Customers—
with buying power

Suppliers—
who stand to gain or lose from your work

Informal change agents—
persons who have great informal influence in the company

Persons who care—
"company types," who sincerely care about what happens,
can be helpful with communication and access to resources

4.6 The Client's Idea of a Timeline

Description

This is a performance consulting project timeline written from the client's point of view.

Explanation

No doubt you are being considered as a problem solver when you are contracted to be a performance consultant. Foremost in the client's mind is a probable date when the problem in fact will be solved. The client will look first at the end date of the timeline. You, on the other hand, will be more concerned with *process* issues: how much time it will take you, alone or in collaboration with others, to make observations, design and conduct interviews, find and analyze documents, determine and verify performance gaps, perhaps travel to other sites, perhaps design and conduct training. In short, the consultant thinks of a timeline in terms of potential person-hours involved in doing work of various sorts. The client thinks of this too, but not in the same way. The client thinks of these as a dollar figure, not as events or processes on a timeline. What's most important to the client is value delivered in a timely fashion with as little disturbance as possible to the client's authority.

Also responsible for paying the consultant, the client is concerned with what the consultant might consider "housekeeping" matters. These are things like project management and financial recordkeeping, timely monitoring, and reporting back to the client or other key persons. Seeing these items on a timeline usually makes a client happy. Here's an example:

September	October	November	December
. Submit budget. . Sign contract.	. Orally report to client . Review client files.	. Identify problem(s). . Generate solutions.	. . Conduct feedback meeting
. Approve documentation forms.	. Observe work flow.	.	. Have exit interview with client.
. Approve project plan.	. Review expenditures with client. .	. Deliver final written report.	.
	. Submit interim invoice.		. Submit final invoice.

What You Already Know That Can Help You

Trainers can start off on the right track when it comes to pleasing the client with a client-sensitive timeline by remembering how important good *training administration* is to you as a trainer. You know how secure it feels to know that someone is paying attention to advertising your training program and creating a good catalog, to registration, to providing for media assistance, to evaluating your delivery and tabulating evaluation results, to billing for your services. Give your client the same kind of careful attention to the business administration of your consulting project.

The Client's Idea of a Timeline

Instructions: As an exercise in client understanding, complete a "Client's Timeline," indicating points on it that seem to be important from the client's point of view. Extend the timeline over as many months as you need for the project. Read down the chart.

September	October	November	December
•	•	•	•
•	•	•	•
•	•	•	•
•	•	•	•
•	•	•	•
•	•	•	•
•	•	•	•
•	•	•	•
•	•	•	•
•	•	•	•

4.7 How to Effectively Modify a Timeline: Yours and Theirs

Description

This is a chart listing elements commonly found in timelines, as well as the options for making modifications to them.

Explanation

Consultants often find themselves in a position to renegotiate, to make modifications, and to clarify various points. Trainers have trouble with this, because training is so carefully structured and timed. Trainers generally are not used to being flexible regarding the design and delivery of training. These checklists should help you see the many possibilities for flexibility in modifying a timeline. Here are a couple of examples:

Instead of this (item 3):
week of 8/10	Observe work flow.

Do this:
8/11	Observe work flow: efficiency of handling paperwork after order placement.
8/13, 8/14	Observe work flow: number of steps and their effectiveness in the order fulfillment process in warehouse operations.

Instead of this (item 7):
7/12	Administer surveys.

Do this:
7/12	Administer surveys.
	a.m. room 208 SJ Mostado
	a.m. room 27 JN Ericson
	p.m. room 208 RC Dockendorff
	p.m. room 27 DK Joyce

What You Already Know That Can Help You

Trainers who review the material on *creative thinking* will find that the process of modification is rooted in the creativity literature. Trainers who have taught workshops in *brainstorming, innovation,* and *creativity* will recognize the importance of mental flexibility. Think first in terms of adding and subtracting; then of inverting, observing, documenting, revising, making something more specific. Think always in terms of what you want and need, as well as what the client wants and needs.

How to Effectively Modify a Timeline: Yours and Theirs

Instructions: Effective modification of a timeline requires flexibility of approach. Remember that consulting is a contractual arrangement between two parties, each of whom has different needs and wants from the project. The best kind of working arrangements consider the contingencies of both parties to the contract. Use this chart to provide ideas for the give and take that consulting requires. Add to the lists to customize them for your own situation.

Elements in Consultant's Timeline	*Ways to Modify*
Complete company culture audit. Observe work flow. Analyze work flow. Get documents from corporate files. Analyze documents. Meet with key players. Set standards/measures. Design and produce surveys. Administer surveys. Create project report. Report to client (content, process, results). Submit expense report. Monitor budget. Submit invoice. Deliver product/service.	1. Greater depth of content 2. More items/points on the timeline 3. Greater specificity 4. Numerical representation of objectives 5. Quality standard for each item 6. Increased or reduced focus on particular categories such as finances, on-site work, feedback sessions, written reports, etc. 7. Addition of names of persons involved at each point 8. Addition of specific dates at each point 9. Addition of narrative overview keyed to each point 10. Addition of narrative overview to the overall timeline 11. _____ _____ 12. _____ _____
Elements in Client's Timeline	
End date "Deliverables" (products, services, changes) Budgets Expense reports Meetings On-site work Measurements Project reports (content, process, results) Invoices	

4.8 How to Organize and Use Data for Contracting

Description

This is a set of steps to follow to organize the data you've collected as you go forward into the contracting process itself.

Explanation

If you're like most people who are about to jump into a consulting project, you have amassed piles of data about the company or organization in which you hope to work. Now your task is to turn all this data into useful information. It's helpful if you can begin at this early stage to identify the real problem; that is, you need to be sure that the "trigger" problem is the real problem. (More often than not, the trigger problem is *not* the real problem.) Use some kind of "piling system" to turn your data into useful information. Here's an example—a graphic representation of the steps on the following page:

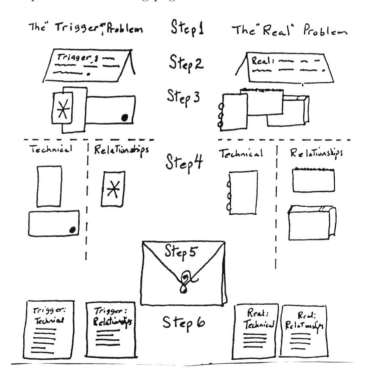

What You Already Know That Can Help You

Trainers understand the value of *design*. Instructional designers and instructors, especially, are accustomed to breaking down the learning experience into segments or *modules* organized around *objectives* for the learner. Instructional designers, when they write courses, build the content of courses and design the processes of teaching and learning according to a system of unfolding lessons of varying difficulty and cumulative interest. In short, instructional designers or instructors have an internalized appreciation for the value of the skills required to turn data into information. Early information categorizing and planning for the use of data can benefit both you and your client.

How to Organize and Use Data for Contracting

Instructions: Follow these steps so that your data become information. Strive to organize the data into categories that help define the issues you believe the project should address. Remember to pay attention to both the business or technical aspects and the relationships of the project. Content and process are both equally important, and data informing each are important to codify early in the contracting phase.

Step 1: Set up two piles:
  (a) One for the "trigger" problem, that is, the problem that brought you and the client together prior to contracting.
  (b) The other for the "real" problem as you begin to define it.

Step 2: Name the piles, being specific and using simple, clear language and short sentences. Don't run ideas together. Make a tent card with these names and place it at the head of each pile so that you can see what you wrote as you organize the data.

Step 3: Place reports and other documentation in the appropriate piles.

Step 4: Within each pile, create subpiles of "technical" and "relationships" and more specifically place the documentation you've collected in the subpiles. Make photocopies of any data that seem to be appropriate to both piles and place duplicate data in any pile that seems right.

Step 5: Review all piles and subpiles for irrelevant data and pull it out. Stash the irrelevant data in a large envelope and put it away. Don't throw it away, however, since your initial assumptions could be wrong and you might need it later in the project.

Step 6: Make adjustments to all piles. When you've done this, make a list of the contents of each pile so that you have an organized summary to work with as you develop the contract.

4.9 How to Write Communication into the Contract

Description

Use these three techniques to expand your own set of communications strategies, particularly at the time of contracting.

Explanation

Behind these three simple consulting communication techniques are rather complex ideas regarding consultant behavior. These are:

1. That consultants are often brought in when things are really bad in terms of relationships as well as when systems or products don't work. Consultants need to recognize that egos get bruised easily, that employees are afraid of losing their jobs or their status, and that the current players have probably tried as hard as they can to make things work. The last thing any employee at any level wants is someone telling them what to do right off the bat. The best and most basic communication skill for a consultant is to ask the right questions and then to listen for the answers. Trainers-turned-consultants often have a very bad time with this because trainers are used to *telling* people things, not *asking*. The trainer's first response is usually to expound, to present, to attempt to influence through personality or expertise. Consultants who do this first generally fall flat on their faces and maybe even never get to the contracting phase of the project.

2. That key players who are freed up to work with a consultant often resent the time away from their "real work"; often there is a hidden conspiracy to withhold information or otherwise resist the consultant's best efforts to uncover problems. The best way to head off some of this is to make an early and strong effort to know the people, what their organizations do, and others in their network of associates. The relationships of a consulting project are just as important as the technical content of the project. Consultants often don't take the time to work on the relationships early in the project; it's more tempting to want to show off your consultant expertise and credentials early in the project. People are your project's most important asset; pay attention to them first.

3. That clients have expectations and familiar ways of receiving information. Find out what these are and follow the client's lead. Don't be tempted to "snow" them.

What You Already Know That Can Help You

Trainers, especially instructors, tend to be naturally good communicators. Those who have been facilitators, not lecturers, are generally gifted communicators by both native competence and by years of training and experience. Transfer of what you know as a trainer about types of *questioning techniques, how to give and receive feedback, how to focus on individuals within a group setting, how to encourage dialogue from even the most reluctant participant, how to prepare handouts and job aids, how to design manuals for ease of use.* All these communication skills can be transferred from the job of trainer to the role of performance consultant. Take stock of what you already know, and apply it in a new way.

How to Write Communication into the Contract

Instructions: Review this list of techniques whenever you need a refresher about communications as a consultant. Trainers are accustomed to the techniques of communication that are appropriate for groups, as in classroom groups or teams. Trainers are accustomed to facilitation techniques that often depend on being fed by the dynamics of groups. This list is attuned to one-to-one communication that generally is characteristic of consulting relationships.

1. *Ask questions and listen* to determine all the motivations for this project. Keep asking as many people as you need to ask to find out whatever is driving this project. Refrain from giving your opinion; concentrate on asking. Hone your skills of probing, using open-ended as well as closed-ended questions, questioning for clarification, questioning to encourage elaboration, etc. Specify reporting sessions in the contract, allowing time for you to ask questions to satisfy all the motivators during the course of the project. Asking and listening are more important than showing and telling.

2. *Identify key players and know their names.* This seems like a simple and obvious thing to do, the very basis of good communication. Make it a point to quickly be able to associate a name with a face even if it means you have to resort to your own private mnemonic devices, cartoons, matrices, or other memory aids. Early in the project get around to meet all key players so that they know your face too. Client employees involved in your consulting engagement are often ill at ease, afraid of being exposed. Do everything you can early in the project to make them professionally comfortable with you. Learn to value every person regardless of position; if they're important to the project, they're equally important to you. Be sure that your contract accommodates data and support materials and that you get an accurate picture of the persons who will be involved with you and that you are guaranteed access to them.

3. *Follow the client's acceptable formats and communication standards.* Remember that only the client can make change because only the client is accountable for his or her work. You have influence as a consultant, but not bottom-line accountability to the company. Your accountability is to your consulting contract. Pay attention to gaining acceptance for your work by providing your consulting products in the client-preferred formats. For example, don't use three-ring binders if they prefer bound books; give status reports in a classroom setting if that's how they like to hear the news. Write these specifics of client expectations into the contract.

4.10 How to Provide in the Contract for Feedback

Description

This checklist is a list of feedback considerations that should be written into the consulting contract. It is built on classic feedback techniques but reflects the special relationship of consultant with the client.

Explanation

These are behavioral guidelines for receiving feedback, for you, the consultant, as you hear what your client has to say.

Guidelines for Receiving Feedback

1. Pay attention; listen actively.
2. Focus on specific points; ask for clarification if you need it.
3. Ask for elaboration of specific points if you need it.
4. Ask for description of specific points so that you know what you might need to change.
5. Accept both negative and positive comments.
6. Ask for the feedback giver's ideas on how to make change.
7. Thank the feedback giver/acknowledge his/her contributions at several times during feedback. It's not easy to give helpful feedback.
8. Don't get defensive; if you've had all you can take, ask to stop and resume later at a specified time.
9. Adopt body language that is accepting and friendly (no crossed arms).
10. During feedback, note any items/ideas that you can act on immediately. Sort out the feedback ideas and act on any that you can. Report back to the feedback giver when you have done so.

Keep in mind also that clients involved in change have many different levels of concern about what's going on, in addition to their potential worries about having a consultant in their midst. Some of these concerns are:

- Personal—how change might be expected to affect him or her personally.
- Managerial or implementative—how to manage or implement the change being proposed; business-related—the consequences of the change or possible long-term effects on the nature of the business, stock value, or cancellation of product lines.

Overtones of some of these concerns can be detected in feedback given to the consultant. A wise consultant takes care of the personal concerns first, then addresses the management or general business concerns. Feedback sessions can tell you a great deal about the business, but always remember to solve the personal problems first.

What You Already Know That Can Help You

Trainers, especially instructors who have been through *pilot testing* of their courses and those who participate in feedback sessions with course evaluators, know the value of feedback that addresses both content and instructional and learning processes. Instructors who do *evaluations beyond the "smiles sheets"* know the value of this kind of "closing the loop."

How to Provide in the Contract for Feedback

Instructions: Refer to this prior to writing the contract for your consulting project.

___ 1. Schedule regular periodic status report meetings in the contract.

___ 2. Specify that feedback from client to you is part of each status report meeting.

___ 3. Specify that feedback is given and received according to a preagreed-on set of guidelines governing the giving and receiving of feedback.

___ 4. Include a blank status report form as part of an appendix to the contract. In it, provide space for written "constraints and concerns" that developed during the time period covered by the status report. In "constraints and concerns" be sure to reflect both your position and the client's position, and in a brief narrative statement describe the problem and possibly the solution. Written narrative often helps clarify communication and reduce the distortions in both sides' perceptions of reality. In this form also provide space for you to tell what you accomplished during this reporting period and your judgment of what still needs to be accomplished during the next reporting period. In these two sections of the form, again give credence to the client's point of view and contributions. Remember, in all dealings on this project, it's a 50/50 endeavor. The written status report is your best complement to oral feedback.

___ 5. Double-check your timeline(s). Be sure that in your detailed timeline you specify the dates on which the status report from you will be presented at the status report meeting. Your best guarantee of good communications is the discipline of regular reporting with all key players involved face to face.

4.11 Checklist for Building Flexibility into the Contract

Description

This is a checklist to be reviewed prior to contracting. It suggests ways to achieve flexibility with honor.

Explanation

Performance consultants can easily get trapped into rigid contracts. This tool helps you write a flexible contract. As you review the six steps, be aware of the underlying contracting foundations inherent in each of these.

1. *Discipline:* Let the contract help you stay focused and disciplined. Remember that you are a guest in this company, an invited outsider. Don't be tempted to act like the CEO; keep your nose out of places you don't belong; learn to channel your efforts within the discipline of the contract(s) you write.

2. *Authenticity:* Be yourself; don't be tempted to tell the clients what they want to hear. Accept the fact that you will have disagreements with the client or other company employees and stakeholders. Learn to manage the yin and the yang—the crisis and the opportunity. Stay above the entanglements of discord; be authentically yourself. Accept discord as a life process whose management you can handle.

3. *Trust:* Mutual respect leading to trust is what sustains a consulting arrangement. At all times seek and value the client's contributions.

4. *Fairness:* Both sides of the contract, client and consultant, must have systems in place to guarantee fairness. Cost is the first place to start.

5. *Collaboration:* Be sure that clients understand their responsibilities regarding this project; use the contract to foster collaboration.

6. *Reasonableness:* In spite of whatever crises brought you and the client together, insist on a reasonable approach to project work. This is true for your expectations of the client as well as the client's expectations of you. A good timeline is one of the foundations for reasonable progress.

What You Already Know That Can Help You

Writing a good contract is probably the most difficult job for a trainer-turned-performance-consultant, largely because trainers don't usually "contract" with trainees. The trainer's model is a service or facilitation model, not a business negotiation model. Perhaps the best preparation for understanding the concept of flexibility in contracting is the trainer's understanding of *objectives in the affective domain* of learning, that is, learning objectives addressing issues of values and attitudes, as contrasted with cognitive objectives or psychomotor objectives. If you as a trainer can transfer what you know about the classification and categorization of affective objectives to the contract flexibility issue, you'll approach the issue correctly.

Checklist for Building Flexibility into the Contract

Instructions: Review this immediately prior to writing your consulting contract.

____ 1. There are two basic kinds of contracts, each related to a phase of the consulting process: the assessment contract and the implementation contract. One project contract can be written to cover both phases, but you give the project more flexibility if you separate them. This is because the activities of assessment are very different from those of implementation, and contingencies are easier to deal with when the two types of activity are separate.

____ 2. Be very clear about assumptions, both yours and the client's. Get all these out in the open before you write anything in a memo of agreement or a contract. Know where you and the client differ, and know where you agree. Document the assumptions on both sides, including the shared assumptions, and date the document. Review it periodically with the client to be sure that the assumptions remain intact as the project goes forward. Disagreement is fine, and in fact allows the project a certain kind of flexibility as both sides anticipate coming together eventually.

____ 3. Make a list of your mutual expectations. Separate the list into "processes" and "outcomes." Agree on these expectations before you put contract words around them. This allows you flexibility whether you meet all expectations or don't. Additional contracts can be written in either case.

____ 4. Provide cost estimates in terms of units—a per-diem consulting fee, per-item scoring, per-page development fee, etc. If assumptions change or time and resources expand, you can still remain within the spirit of the contract.

____ 5. Write into the contract or letter of agreement specific decision points for the client. Make it clear that you intend to support and influence ideas and action, but the client is the final decision maker. This allows you flexibility in modifying the timeline and nature of deliverables, depending on what the client decides.

____ 6. In most timelines, two-week intervals are acceptable. You'll maintain flexibility if you set your milestones at two-week intervals, even if you expect to be able to deliver a product or service within a shorter time.

4.12 If ... Then Chart for Getting Out of Contracting before You Get In

Description

This chart suggests actions you can take to prevent contracting disasters and to get out of consulting before you enter a hopelessly difficult arrangement.

Explanation

Persons new to consulting, and perhaps particularly trainers-turned-consultants, often approach the new business of consulting trying to be needed, wanted, and of service. This is the wrong mindset, primarily because in this frame of mind you tend to be willing to accept a less than 50/50 deal. You tend not to be assertive in stating your expectations and needs; you tend to think that, if you make a mistake or an omission early in the process, you can cover for it or make it up later. Remember that consultants are sales persons and problem solvers, not service personnel or scapegoats.

Consultants need to remember that it's okay not to get a contract if that contract situation is so fraught with snakes, wild beasts, and landmines that you'll never come out of it unscathed. Put on your sales person cap and go for the next contract. It's important to stick to your professional standards, even before the contract is written—or be prepared to fall back into a trainer's way of doing business. Here's what some of the experts say:

> When you are irreparably stuck with the client, you need to say, "We are having a hard time reaching agreement, perhaps now is not a good time to do this work," or "I would suggest that we not begin this project, since we can't seem to agree on how to proceed." Using your own style and own words, end the contracting process and cut your losses.
>
> Peter Block, *Flawless Consulting* (1981), p. 75.

> If the client is adamant in wanting a program (such as training) and resistant to the questioning process, be prepared to return to the traditional training approach and provide the training that is requested, or be prepared to say no to the client's request.
>
> Dana Gaines Robinson and James C. Robinson, *Performance Consulting* (1995), p. 248.

What You Already Know That Can Help You

Instructional designers recognize the if ... then chart as one example of *analytical thinking*, similar to the reasoning processes a trainer goes through when doing a training *needs assessment* or identifying gaps in learner behavior from "what is" to "what should be." If ... then reasoning is a mental model that training designers find useful in developing course content. It also applies to the *systems thinking* that trainers engage in when diagnosing and building organizational learning.

If ... Then Chart for Getting Out of Contracting before You Get In

Instructions: Review this chart before your critical contracting meeting with the client. Use it to remind yourself of the danger signs regarding the impending contract.

If	Then
• You can't figure out who the client is /	• Postpone the contracting meeting until the client makes it obvious.
• The client is reluctant to state clearly his/her expectations /	• Suggest that this will be a two-way deal; put one of your expectations on the table and suggest that the client match it; continue one for one until you have a 50/50 statement.
• The client is nervous and expresses concern over his/her loss of control /	• Try to reassure the client that you expect to exert influence, not control; that you have access but not authority; that you don't want his/her job; that you hope to collaborate; that you know your limits.
• Your freedom of movement or access to data is constrained from the start /	• Ask the client directly why this lack of trust before the project begins; probe until you uncover the reasons and attempt to build trust in *you* so that issues of movement and access are resolved before contracting.
• There really is not enough money to do the project to your professional standards /	• Cut your losses and don't enter into a contract for this project; redefine the project into several smaller ones, giving the client the option of choosing a project of lesser scope.
• None of these strategies works /	• Bow out gracefully.

Chapter 5

Analyzing Performance

Step 2: Define core processes.

Step 3: Analyze organizational performance.

Step 4: Analyze individual performance.

This chapter concentrates on the process of analysis. Within its pages are the three critical steps to begin performance consulting once your contract is signed. It is important at this early stage of work to stay focused on analysis tasks without prejudicing your work toward solutions. As in creative thinking, brainstorming, and the mindset of innovation, practice deferring judgment during all analysis processes. Save solution finding for later in the performance-consulting project; concentrate now on looking hard at the nature of performance.

The disciplines of analysis are largely descriptive answers to the questions:

- What am I seeing?

- What shall I look for?

- What are the parameters of?

- What are the relationships among?

- How many?

- Who?

Such questions yield specific definitions, descriptions, classifications, taxonomies, frames, patterns, categories, numbers, and names. Within the range of consultant performance, analysis comes at the very lowest end; at the highest end comes evaluation when the consultant and client determine whether interventions have made a difference. Within an organizational systems framework, analysis begins the input phase of the organizational loop; again, evaluation completes the loop with its outputs that then feed back into more analysis as progress continues. In the instructional systems design framework for creating learning experiences, analysis starts the process and, again, evaluation of results completes it.

Analysis must be kept "pure" so that the descriptions it produces are as valid and complete as possible. Tools in this chapter help you stay focused on doing analysis, that is, on sticking to a commitment to the all-important beginning of performance consulting without getting bogged down or jumping the gun to solutions. Fourteen separate tools are included here. They follow the format begun in Chapter 4. These tools are spread over Steps 2, 3, and 4.

Tools in Chapter 5

STEP 2

Step 2: Define core processes.
Begin by defining what
this company does, that is,
the processes by which the
employees and the systems
work together for common goals.

5.1 Core Processes

This chart suggests several representations of core processes and ideas for working with your client to identify them.

Explanation

Process is the all-important variable in performance. What is going on, what is happening, what makes this business run—these are the primary questions to ask of your client as you develop a list of essential ways in which people and systems interact in this company. A productive way to start generating this list is to encourage the client, or client team, to think in terms of action—use "ing" words in making the list, for example, *serving* customers rather than customer service, *producing* rather than production, *monitoring* quality rather than quality assurance. Getting people to think in terms of action words early in the project is helpful in generating ideas. Thinking actively also tends to help people see how both organizational influences and individual influences relate to the process you've identified. This kind of action-oriented, process thinking forms the foundation of many later steps in the performance-consulting endeavor. If you're having trouble getting started here, take a look at the company telephone directory or organization chart for an overview of how the company is organized; translate what you see structurally into a list of processes for getting work done. Then read between the lines and add processes such as managing projects, communicating across functions, disseminating critical information, etc.

What You Already Know That Can Help You

Trainers who have worked in a corporate training center, at a corporate university, or for a vendor of training services or products have a broad perspective of the range of jobs in a company. You have a good feel for this because of the range of persons coming through a training operation. If you've neglected to be interested in this broad view, take a few moments to review *enrollment data* from your training administrator. You'll quickly refresh or add to your memory about the kinds of jobs that make a company work. Jobs with people in them translate into processes. Trainers who have worked in management training and in training for teams have an excellent set of skills for working with clients to carry out Step 2. Refresh your skills in *asking questions*, in *active listening*, in *facilitating group process*, and in *brainstorming*—all areas of expertise in which these kinds of trainers excel and all needed in Step 2.

Core Processes

Instructions: Refer to this chart before you design client contact time for analyzing performance. Choose an approach or several approaches to collaborative time together; know exactly what you're doing so that you can control the hours you spend in this analysis activity. Remember, time is money in consulting work.

Structural Approach to Process

❏ Use company structural documents (e.g., organization chart, telephone directory, payroll categories, etc.) to suggest how work is done in the various parts of the company. Make a list of key processes within each category you choose to use. Use "ing" words in your lists (e.g., accounting, engineering, conducting research, managing inventory, training, hiring employees, etc.).

❏ Realize that the structural approach analyzes the current situation and is based on current and past decisions about how the company should be structured.

❏ Continue subcategorizing your terms, refining the processes demonstrated in your company (e.g., hiring employees/reviewing resumes/interviewing/placing/orienting new employees, etc.). Set a standard of some level of detail.

❏ Assign a weight to each process representing the degree of its contribution to the company's uniqueness and competitive advantage; from this weighting, determine which processes are indeed the core processes.

Futurist Approach to Process

❏ Engage your client team in discussing what the company will have to do well in five years. Put a future orientation on developing this process list.

❏ Focus on the processes required to create, sustain, and protect knowledge.

❏ Relate any process defined to the company's strengths, uniqueness, and specialized products and services. Think in terms of the most value for customers now and within the next five years.

❏ Refine the list through scenario planning, brainstorming, and hypothesizing.

Benchmarking

❏ After identifying several core processes, suggest a formal benchmarking project to determine how other companies compare with your company on each of these processes. Look at things like acquiring customers, filling orders, making sales.

❏ Benchmarking can be expensive, due to visitors' fees and time away from the job. Be sure that you know exactly what processes are the important ones to benchmark before you set up trips to other companies.

❏ Benchmarking is an experience-based information dissemination process. This kind of approach can help motivate clients toward change and help clients see what kinds of processes they can adapt to their own change efforts.

❏ Benchmarking in the real world is often more helpful to clients than following process models.

5.2 Core Competencies

Description

This checklist is a list of considerations in defining core competencies. It provides insight into both the human resource and the workplace politics aspects of competency.

Explanation

Identifying and defining core competencies follows the identification of core processes, but it is more difficult. Its goal is to identify and define the confluence of individual competencies that make the company best in class, the most feared or savvy competitor—a representation of the company's unique human resources and knowledge advantages. Defining core competencies is a recognition that the whole is greater than the sum of its parts. Making a list of best practices is a good place to start. It might take some "evolving" of your consulting activities before these core competencies can be identified. You'll begin to think about them, however, as you refine your definition of the company's core processes. A classic discussion of core competencies is found in *Competing for the Future* by Gary Hamel and C. K. Prahalad (Boston: Harvard Business School Press, 1994, particularly Chaps. 9 and 10).

What You Already Know That Can Help You

K,S,As—knowledge, skills, and attitudes. Anyone who's taken educational psychology courses remembers Bloom's taxonomies of educational objectives (1956). Bloom and his colleagues at the University of Chicago for several decades flooded the teaching and learning community with hierarchical representations of objectives for learners. They believed that some kinds of things had to be learned, that is, mastered, before other things could be learned. They understood that learning is multidimensional, that it is affected by the style preferences of learners, and that various tasks fit more appropriately in one category or another. Their work led to advances in the craft of designing instruction, and spawned whole professions of curriculum designers and instructional technologists. Their influence persists today. The concept of domains of knowledge is one of the important underpinnings of analysis of core competencies.

In more recent times, works such as Howard Gardner's *Frames of Mind: The Theory of Multiple Intelligences* echo Bloom's train of thought. On page x (1985) Gardner defines intelligence as "the ability to solve problems, or to create products, that are valued within one or more cultural settings." He elaborates this idea by suggesting that intelligence is actually made up of seven different intelligences and that individuals have some of all of these in varying proportions. They are linguistic, musical, logical-mathematical, spatial, bodily-kinesthetic, inter, and intrapersonal intelligence. Gardner's work is important because he adds the value component to the categorization. A newer work, *The Knowledge-Creating Company* by Nonaka and Takeuchi (1995) makes a convincing case for the investigation of "tacit" knowledge, more akin to intuitive know-how. These are the sources of theories behind the definition of "core competencies."

Core Competencies

Instructions: Review this checklist before you initiate discussion with your client about core competencies.

___ 1. Stay focused on identifying and defining. Don't get off on the tangent of causes or of problem solving. Remember the old saw, "Pay now or pay later." Make every effort to do a good job of analysis. It saves you time, money, and aggravation later.

___ 2. Adopt a holistic perspective. Think in terms of tacit knowledge, accumulated wisdom that drives action, intuition, savvy, and smarts.

___ 3. Focus on value. Relate the corporate knowledge, skills, and attitudes exhibited by top performers to a dollars-and-cents value to the company and ultimately to the customer.

___ 4. Manage the politics. If you are facilitating a client group or team discussion, be aware that each individual wants to make sure that his or her job is viewed as "core." Structure your client sessions so that everyone has equal opportunity to be heard, to contribute, to criticize, and to ask and answer questions. This could take weeks.

___ 5. Encourage cross-functional thinking. You are seeking a definition of the corporate competencies, or the combined unique capacities of individual employees, that keep this company at the head of the pack. Examples might be the way we seek and disseminate information, our intellectual property protections (licenses, patents, copyrights), our recipe for soft drink (Coca-Cola), power trains (Honda), 20 well-placed employees who can "feel it in their bones," etc. Abstract the core competencies from the tangle of position, job, product, leadership, budget, marketing, longevity, etc.

___ 6. Don't fall into the trap of sounding like the annual report, which features assets, capital spending and investment, and shareholder value. Concentrate instead on customer value and employee smarts. Core competencies are related to individual performance, and this can be improved for an even greater contribution to value in the future; tangible assets and capital are not necessarily related to improving individual performance for the long term.

___ 7. Continue the process of definition by making sublists of intelligences, skills, attitudes, or values that contribute to each core competency that you define. Set yourself up in this analysis process to be able later to develop a plan for magnifying the core competencies you've identified. Get more of them, build on or enhance the ones you have, recognize and reward individuals who have them, transfer and institutionalize them throughout the company, preserve and protect them.

5.3 Use of PERT Network to Describe Core Processes

Description

This graphic representation of events and activities can be useful in describing interrelationships between and within core processes.

Explanation

PERT stands for Program Evaluation and Review Technique. It is a network graphic, meant to show interrelationships. It was designed to graph activities and events. It can be adapted to show process interrelationships. The PERT network has been useful as a planning tool. In the context of performance analysis, PERT can be a tool that adds to your skills of description and explanation.

The following example illustrates its use:

This PERT network graphs the core process of informing the public. The timeline at the bottom of the page can be described in any way that's useful—a month, a quarter, a year, etc. Fill it out before you begin. Each circle represents a subprocess that contributes to the success of the core process. Connecting lines represent activities that are going on between the subprocesses. All circles are represented by a number that indicates the order in which these subprocesses must occur. In this case, the numbers represent:

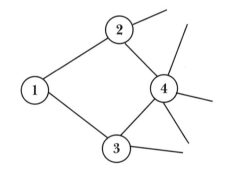

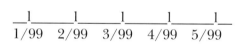

1. Research grant becomes available.
2. Creative team meets.
3. Engineering team meets.
4. R&D director and production director talk to staff via TV and hold press conference immediately after the staff talk.

An interesting exercise is to develop a PERT network representing each of the previously defined core processes. Create each network on the same timeline, for easier comparison when you've finished all of them. Taking a vertical look at all networks against the timeline lets you quickly see bottlenecks—where you are understaffed or unprepared for what must come next. Often, the next phase after analysis—that is, diagnosis—is facilitated by a carefully prepared PERT network. When you can both isolate and relate subprocesses that contribute to a core process, you have a better chance of being accurate in your analysis.

What You Already Know That Can Help You

Trainers who have operated under ISD, the *instructional systems design* framework, with its emphasis on feedback, feel comfortable constructing networks. Management trainers recognize PERT as a classic planning tool.

Use of PERT Network to Describe Core Processes

Instructions: In this graphic, all circles are connected. Each circle represents an event; each connecting line represents activities occurring over time. Use this graphing technique to represent a single process or the work of an entire team, department, or company.

Sample of a Completed PERT Network

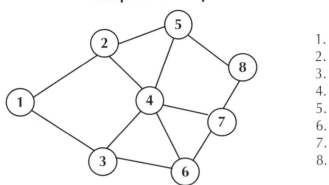

1.
2.
3.
4.
5.
6.
7.
8.

Timeline _____

Construct your own PERT network, using circles and connecting lines along a timeline that you define. Identify the circles in a list for easy reference. Use as many circles as you need to define the process(es) that you observe.

1.
2.
3.
4.
5.
6.
7.
8.
9.
10.
11.
12.

Timeline _____

5.4 Ways to Look at and Use Mission Statements

Description

This checklist contains ideas about how to analyze and use corporate mission statements.

Explanation

"If you don't know where you're going, any road will get you there." This is a familiar expression in management and organizational studies. It applies to analyzing performance. As a consultant, you can't afford to travel "any road." This is not a leisurely drive in the country just for the fun of it. A better approach is to know where you're going, that is, to know where the company intends to go.

The first place to look for this information is the corporate mission statement. This, of course, may be called by a variety of names. Some of the common ones are statement of values, statement of principles, our credo, our quest for excellence, vision statement, corporate direction. By whatever name it is called, this statement usually gives a clear description in a few words of where the company is going. It also usually articulates the values and beliefs by which the company intends to operate. The mission statement is a good document from which to extract ideas and terminology to incorporate into your descriptions of core processes and competencies. Studying the mission statement can help clarify process, goals, beliefs, etc. A good example of the clarifying effect of a mission statement is the first statement in Avis Rent-A-Car's "The Avis Quest for Excellence." It says, "At Avis Rent-A-Car, our business is renting cars; our mission is total customer satisfaction." (Jones and Kahaner, 1995, p. 12) In defining Avis's core process, you would focus on the business of renting cars; in defining its core competencies, you would focus on factors that enable the company to achieve its mission.

What You Already Know That Can Help You

Most trainers have had some experience in developing mission statements, even if this experience has been limited to the *mission of the training operation*. Those who have been management trainers probably also have taught units of instruction on how to create a mission statement in management seminars. Many employees carry with them a *wallet card* with the company's mission statement on it. Review the format and content of those mission statements you have known in the past; the ones you'll analyze for your client will probably have some of the same characteristics.

Ways to Look at and Use Mission Statements

Instructions: Use this as a guide to reading and using corporate mission statements as input to defining a company's core processes.

____ 1. Look for a clear definition of the company's business.

____ 2. Look for a clear statement of mission, a strong, focused desire to arrive by a straight and narrow path to a valued place.

____ 3. Look for statements of belief.

____ 4. Look for programmatic ways in which the company says it will carry out the mission.

____ 5. Look for realistic relationships between the mission statement and the stated means to accomplish the mission.

____ 6. Compare the variables in the mission statement with definitions of core processes and core competencies derived through previous discussions.

____ 7. Design a chart or matrix that relates the mission to the process variables.

____ 8. Audit the mission statement for believability, credibility, potential for positive action, motivational effect, and other criteria you devise. Describe what you find.

____ 9. Look for unique terms and phrases that help to define the company; use these in your own definition of the company's core processes.

STEP 3

**Step 3: Analyze
organizational performance.**
Continue analysis by focusing on the
organizational variables
surrounding individual performance.
Consider the physical and psychological
work environment, control and participation,
information, structure, support,
and systems.

5.5 Key Factors in Productivity

Description

This formula for productivity includes a number of organizational performance variables.

Explanation

Organizational performance, as well as individual performance, is affected by productivity. People have a fuzzy understanding about what productivity is and isn't. This tool is designed to help you define productivity in quantifiable terms so that you can measure it.

Many factors contribute to organizational productivity. The simplest definition of productivity is the ratio of output to input, expressed as a fraction:

$$\text{Productivity} = \frac{\textbf{Output}}{\textbf{Input}}$$

In organizational terms, this means that corporate resources—information, employees, buildings, material, inventory, etc.—have to be managed and used to maintain a favorable balance of outputs over inputs. When the cost of inputs, such resources, is greater than the output they produce, the ratio becomes imbalanced and productivity falls. Assigning numbers to the fraction illustrates this effect:

$$\text{Productivity} = \frac{\textbf{Output}}{\textbf{Input}} = \frac{4}{8} = 0.5 \quad \text{or} \quad \text{Productivity} = \frac{\textbf{Output}}{\textbf{Input}} = \frac{8}{4} = 2$$

Productivity of 2 is far better than productivity of 0.5 (1/2). When input variables exceed the output they generate, productivity suffered, as in the case of the 0.5 figure. When the expenditure of input variables is controlled so that output is far greater than the input, productivity soars, as in the case of the ratio of 2. Your analysis of organizational performance helps to uncover the input variables that figure in a calculation of productivity and ultimately to define organizational performance.

What You Already Know That Can Help You

Training administrators and instructors can relate to the "need to know" versus "nice to know" controversy. Experienced classroom instructors know the pain of having trainees who either "know it all" or who really don't need to know what you're attempting to teach them. You know when you are wasting resources, especially the trainees' time and money, not to mention their mental health and the time it took to prepare a course that was off-target. Trainees don't like to pay for training that is excessive on the "input" part of the equation. This kind of organizational performance analysis is like pinpointing what should be taught to whom or analyzing a course for relevance.

Key Factors in Productivity

Instructions: Keeping the productivity equation in mind, take a hard look at the many factors in organizational life that affect how the organization as a whole uses its resources. Search especially for the input variables. Use this chart listing typical organizational performance variables to guide your analysis. Take any item from section B and reference it to any item(s) in section A of the chart. Aim to set up your factors in such a way that numbers can be assigned to them, for eventual calculation of an organizational productivity number. Remember that productivity, a quantitative measure, can have a significant effect on performance, a qualitative measure. Add more items to either section of the chart as need indicates.

$$\text{Productivity} = \frac{\text{Output}}{\text{Input}}$$

A.
Sample Quantitative Indices

profit	intervals	absenteeism	items rejected
margin	time	turnover rate	safety violations/accidents
sales	repeat business	items of inventory	opinion survey results
cost	returns	cost of litigation	payroll costs
errors	complaints	items produced	rewards and bonuses

B.
Sample Organizational Variables

_____	1. hiring (time and cost)	_____	12. scrap and waste
_____	2. orientation (time and cost)	_____	13. accuracy
_____	3. training (time and cost)	_____	14. reliability
_____	4. time and cost to develop	_____	15. communication channels
_____	5. equipment failures	_____	16. experimentation and testing
_____	6. missteps in policy implementation	_____	17. on-the-job learning
_____	7. procedural or production reruns	_____	18. self-study
_____	8. information requests	_____	19. dissemination
_____	9. raw material	_____	20. distribution
_____	10. customer service calls	_____	21. overhead
_____	11. monitoring and feedback	_____	22. chain of command

5.6 How to Go for the Numbers: Using Histograms and Pareto Charts

Description

These simple bar charts show how to represent organizational variables in numerically terms. They are useful in illustrating your analytical work as a basis for dialogue with others.

Explanation

A *histogram* is a frequency count rotated 180 degrees to stand up straight. It is a bar graph showing spread of variation by recording and representing how often each measurement occurs. To construct a useful histogram, generally, at least 50 measurements are suggested as a baseline. The histogram has two axes, a vertical and a horizontal, each representing a number of something: for example, the number of absences versus months; the number of items versus length; the number of responses versus minutes to respond; the number of grievances versus attorneys' fees; etc. A finished histogram, like a frequency count, generally resembles a normal curve (bell curve).

A *Pareto chart* is also a bar graph, but it goes one step beyond simple frequency counting. Its purpose is to indicate the rank order of importance. Useful in showing the relative importance of various elements of a situation or process, it is often used to suggest where resources should be targeted. The first step is to decide which variable to analyze and to represent it on the horizontal (x) axis across the bottom: for example, projected sources of sales for this book (trade sales, direct mail, discount megastores, international, etc.). On the vertical axis (y), place numbers in plausible intervals representing the numbers of or dollar amounts of sales, or the dollar amounts of favorable margin. Arrange the bars in descending order of "goodness." Bars on a Pareto chart would show clearly where the most effort should be directed. In this example, the chart shows where the best sales and marketing effort should be directed for maximum earnings.

Both the histogram and Pareto chart are simple graphic representations that can show quantified performance variables in relationship. They are analytical tools for graphically representing process and organizational variables.

What You Already Know That Can Help You

Most trainers on the job today have been steeped in the *quality movement*, with its emphasis on monitoring processes, quantification of organizational relationships, use of graphical tools for representing information, and providing feedback to stakeholders. These two bar charts are useful tools for translating these quality movement emphases into the performance analysis arena. You've probably taught them in quality workshops. Contact the American Society for Quality [(ASQ), Milwaukee, WI 800/952-6587] for more information about quality tools and its publications list. A simple explanation of both the histogram and Pareto chart, and many other graphics, can be found in a 3×5-inch pocket paperback booklet, *Waste Chasers* (Conway Quality, Inc., Nashua, NH 800-359-0099).

How to Go for the Numbers: Using Histograms and Pareto Charts

Instructions: Using the quantitative data you've collected, construct either or both of these simple bar charts to represent your findings. Aim for at least 50 measurements to assure validity and good statistical performance. Name each axis, identifying the processes or conditions you want to correlate. Construct your own charts below.

Sample Histogram

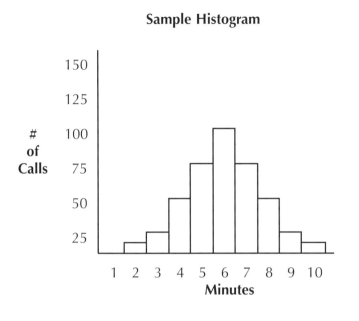

Sample Pareto Chart

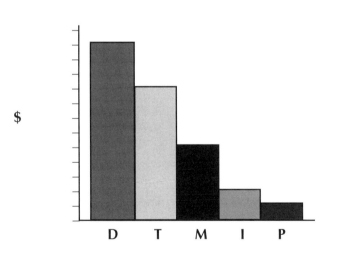

5.7 Analyzing Team Performance

Description

These lists suggest categories of team structure and function that could be the focus of analysis early in your consulting work.

Explanation

Teams at work are a fact of life. Companies have customized their definitions of team, however, and what's a team to one company is not necessarily a team to another. As a performance consultant doing organizational analysis, you must be sure that you understand exactly what "team" means in the client company. You have to separate the process of analysis from that of diagnosis.

We begin with issues in analysis. (Diagnosis is reserved for Chapter 6.) Analytical tasks regarding teams entail definition, categorization, and differentiation. Analyzing team performance is complicated because teams have been created both as a defense against or a response to problems or dire predictions, as well as a proactive, planned organizational structure aligned with business goals. Teams have been formed with great sloppiness as well as with great care. Teams have been built because management saw them as an avenue to accomplish what it couldn't within a currently immobilized or outdated organizational structure, as well as because management truly believed in employee empowerment. "Survivor sickness" after downsizing has impeded the work of teams, and lack of training in communication skills has jeopardized good teamwork intentions. On the other hand, love of learning, adequate support, and an experimentation mentality have all enabled teams to excel. Start the process of team performance analysis with serious defining tasks.

Lists on Tool 5.7 are meant to suggest the kinds of things to look for as you analyze teams. The lists are tip-of-the-iceberg suggestions, designed to spark your own imagination, memory, and knowledge about what it takes to make a team work.

What You Already Know That Can Help You

Trainers who have been schooled in instructional design theories and techniques probably have studied Benjamin Bloom's definitions of analysis (1956), Robert Gagne's conditions of learning (1979), and more recently the work of cognitivists Donald Norman (1993) and John Seely Brown (1997) or Hilary McLellan, ed. (1996). The field of *cognitive psychology*, particularly educational psychology, is full of ideas and approaches to analysis as one of the fundamental "things that make us smart" (Norman's phrase). Bloom, for example, says that analysis can be applied to elements, relationships, procedures, roles, and organizing principles; Brown and McLellan say that true knowledge is "situated" in context and that learning advances through collaborative social action. A review of the work of some of these authors gives you the smarts you need to undertake the in-depth and complicated analysis of team performance.

Analyzing Team Performance

Instructions: Use these lists as a source of reference and inspiration. Develop your own lists of structures and features of teams that need identification and clarification before you can begin problem identification and solution. As you collect information about teams in your client company, prepare some kind of documentation form for this information so that it will be useful to you as you go forward into diagnosis and interventions. Several documentation ideas are also included for reference and inspiration.

Team Name _____	Team Needs	Team Metrics
Purpose _____ Roles _____ Responsibilities _____ Operational guidelines _____ Boundaries _____ Funding _____ Nonfinancial support _____ Communication _____	Access Visibility/PR Removal of obstacles Ground rules Job design Money Advocacy Leadership Empowerment	Timeliness Relevance Sufficiency Necessity Usefulness Speed Accuracy

Documentation Ideas

A. Make a chart listing terms (items in the list) down the side. Across the top, list columns labeled *Definition, Key Contact Person,* and *Metric.* Fill in the chart as you do your analysis.

B. Make a chart listing terms (items in the list) down the side. Across the top, list only one column labeled *Examples.* Allow plenty of space between items so that you can list descriptive examples of each item.

C. Code the items in the list that you have analyzed in some bipolar way, so that your documentation form enables you to follow up. For example, code each analyzed item with a plus or a minus, a present or absent, a clear or unclear, or any other yes/no kind of quick reference point for further work.

5.8 Use of the Flowchart to Describe Processes in Motion

Description

The flowchart has traditionally been used to represent organizational processes. It is appropriate for either large-view processes or small-view subprocesses or procedures. A flowchart focuses on process inputs, outputs, and decisions. It also shows the flow of primary operations as well as loops away from the main system flow.

Explanation

Remember that you are still in analysis mode, and that naming, or identifying, operations in an orderly fashion, is what you are doing when you construct a flowchart. The two unique features of a flowchart are (1) its emphasis on the orderly flow of operations, and (2) its inclusion of decision points in its representation. Often the fact of naming the decision point within operational flow leads you to swift and accurate problem diagnosis later. In the flowchart, however, stick to *naming* the elements in the process and clarifying the operations that you are observing and documenting.

On the following page, the beginnings of two sample flowcharts are provided to illustrate the use of flowcharting in both the large-view and the small-view analysis. Use these as models when you draw your own flowcharts.

Example A	**Example B**
This large-view flowchart illustrates the beginning representations of the process of finding a Chief Knowledge Officer (CKO).	This small-view flowchart takes one of the processes from the large-view flowchart and charts only the subprocess.

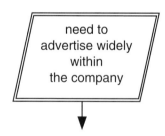

What You Already Know That Can Help You

Trainers who have been instructors or instructional designers know that both content and process are important in successful learning. Instructors spend a lot of time and energy getting the process of teaching right, honing their facilitation skills and techniques for managing group dynamics. Instructional designers design "process" into courses to support the content. Trainers are familiar with structuring objectives in a certain way, by organizing content into units of instruction, by adjusting timing, and by choosing presentation vehicles appropriate to one kind of content or another—all with the goal of helping the process to work in support of the content. Flowcharting is akin to this kind of trainer's process in the delivery and design of instruction. As in training, getting the process right is critical to success.

Use of the Flowchart to Describe Processes in Motion

Instructions: Identify the process that you will represent in the flowchart. Determine its trigger, or starting, point. Using standard flowchart symbols, name each operation and decision, connecting all operations with arrow lines showing the direction of the flow of the process. These are the most commonly used symbols:

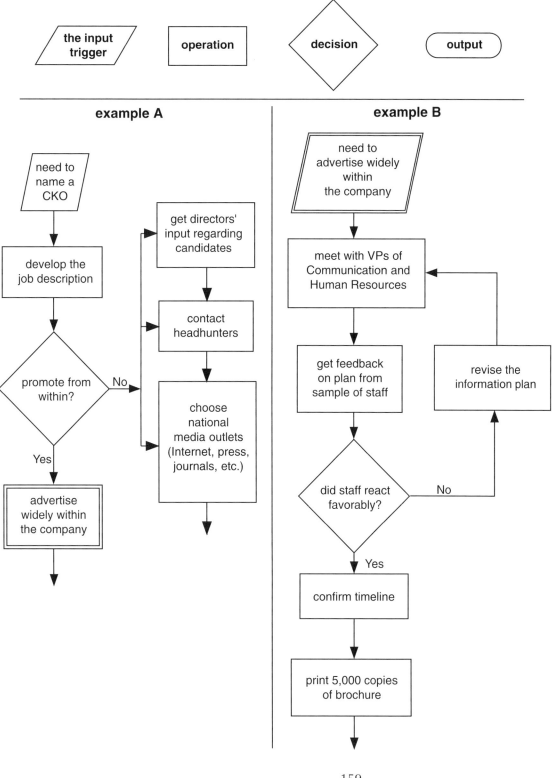

STEP 4

Step 4: Analyze individual performance.
Complete the three basic performance
analysis steps by concentrating now on
analyzing individual performance.
This step describes the actual
performance situation at the level of
the individual employee. It comes after
analysis of organizational performance
because organizational analysis often
provides information that brings
individual performance into clearer focus.

5.9 Job Design Checklist

Description

Refer to this checklist when you have completed organizational analysis.

Explanation

The beginning stages of individual performance analysis inevitably center around the idea of "job"—a person's job, job description, job responsibilities, job performance, job advancement, job status, etc. A *job* is loosely defined as what an individual does for an employer in exchange for pay. How all jobs in a company are configured is generally referred to as *job design*. Job design is a particularly important concept today because of mergers, acquisitions, downsizings, outsourcing, and other structural changes that cause jobs to take on more or less meaning and expectation with new ways of working and new work to be done. Cross-functional work and empowerment of front-line workers have also contributed to confusion in how jobs are structured across organizations and the company as a whole. The trend of hierarchies giving way to teams also tends to cloud the definition of "job."

Numerous writers today speak about what it takes to be a knowledge-based company, especially what companies must do to support and stimulate the creation of individual knowledge. Nonaka and Takeuchi (1995), for example—in *The Knowledge-Creating Company,* the book that started the "knowledge" dialogue in the business press—say that the individual *creates* and the organization *amplifies* the knowledge created by individuals. The organization does this by fostering a "shared context" in which people at work share experiences, dialogue, and discuss, in addition to observing each other's work. They suggest that the dynamic of work-focused relationships within this shared context facilitates the transformation of personal knowledge into organizational knowledge (pp. 239–240).

Individuals relate to work through jobs, and job design is the useful organizational outline that keeps individuals focused on their place in the structure of the workplace and on their relationships with other individuals in other jobs. Performance consultants today are well advised to spend some time analyzing the actual job design of the client workplace before launching into analysis of individual performance. Tool 5.9 gives you some guidance.

What You Already Know That Can Help You

Technical trainers have generally been schooled in the practices of job analysis and task analysis. Many *government trainers* and trainers who have worked for *unions* and for *accrediting agencies* have also mastered the skills of job analysis. These are similar to the skills needed for analysis of the broader job design. Many *human resources generalists* and *organizational development* specialists have displayed the skills required for analysis of job design. To be successful, you need a job skills orientation within an organizational perspective.

Job Design Checklist

Instructions: Review this checklist before you begin analyzing individual performance. Use this checklist as a guide to defining the "shared context" of jobs in this company. Remember: This is still an analysis process meant to describe your findings.

- ❏ 1. Do job titles reflect what individuals do at work?
- ❏ 2. How many persons hold jobs with the same title?
- ❏ 3. Do the organizations in which job titles reside seem able to support those jobs? Do job titles belong there?
- ❏ 4. Are the job functions within each job title reasonable, clear, and nonredundant?
- ❏ 5. Are the responsibilities of job holders clearly spelled out?
- ❏ 6. Are organizational support structures for jobs in place and functioning well? (computer systems, procedures, management, supervision, performance standards, evaluation processes, clerical help, information, etc.)
- ❏ 7. Does the job design encourage sharing and learning on the job? What evidence supports or negates this?
- ❏ 8. Are performance standards in place equally for all job titles?
- ❏ 9. Does each job title have an equal opportunity to succeed or fail?
- ❏ 10. Is performance monitoring, feedback, and opportunity for corrective action part of all job titles? Are they part of the overall job design?
- ❏ 11. Is the performance evaluation process consistent across all jobs?

5.10 Job Analysis

Description

This chart contains several techniques for analyzing an individual job. Such analysis is important in establishing performance standards associated with the analysis of an individual's job performance.

Explanation

A person's performance in a job depends on many things. Among the most common are (1) the match between the true nature of the job and the person's expectations, (2) the comparison between an expert's performance in the same job and the individual's performance, and (3) the extent to which a person advances his or her own sense of self-worth through the job. Job analysis looks at both the components of the job and the traits and skills of the person who holds the job.

The chart in Tool 5.10 presents issues and suggests analysis techniques in each of these three areas. The first analysis uses a people-data-things job description; the second analysis involves the input of expert performers; and the third analysis uses introspection and self-assessment by the job incumbent. Each performance analysis approach is distinct from the others; within each there could be a range of data-gathering forms, surveys, interview schedules, and questioning techniques. The chart is provided as an example of three different approaches to job analysis. It is up to you, the performance consultant, to devise your own plans and documentation forms.

What You Already Know That Can Help You

Instructional designers who have done *training needs assessments* have typically done job analysis with training in mind. When a training needs assessment or front-end analysis uncovered a skills or knowledge gap in a job, the instructional designer got to work creating instructional activities around objectives to bridge the gaps. Doing a performance analysis is similar, but training is not necessarily the preferred mindset. A training bias can get in the way of performance analysis; however, training needs assessment skills can be put to work in a performance analysis situation.

Job Analysis

Instructions: Refer to this chart for ideas in conducting a job analysis.

People-Data-Things Job Analysis

An objective look at the actual nature of the job is provided by listing the duties and responsibilities of the job in three columns: people duties, data duties, and things duties. Ask the person in the job to write down as many duties he or she can think of that truly represent the job. Organize the list into three columns (people, data, things). Count the number of total entries and equate that total to 100%. Then determine the percentage of the job spent in each column. Verify the job profile that emerges with the person in the job. Examples in each category are: *people duties* = supervise, coordinate, facilitate, present; *data duties* = calculate, enter data, analyze data, monitor; *things duties* = repair, lift, assemble, operate.

Expert Input

Most people want to do a good job at work. Many people enjoy the challenge of working toward a standard, measuring themselves against either their own previous performance or what they understand expert performance to be in the job. Often a job analysis based on the expert's input to standards can be helpful to others in the same job. The expert can be interviewed using a structured questionnaire about the critical tasks of the job, or asked to complete a checklist of essential cognitive—or other—skills that he or she believes are necessary for peak performance. Such skills might include number facility, recall from memory, speed, written expression, organization, small muscle coordination. Job analysis from the expert's point of view can help to clarify standards of performance for everyone.

Self-Assessment

Individual performance very much depends on the individual's psychological fit to the job. A self-assessment job survey can yield information that can help the performance consultant guide individuals through productive career planning and ultimately to higher performance. Self-assessments generally focus on "knowing yourself"—on being able to articulate on a survey form or tape cassette the answers to questions such as, "Do I work best in groups or alone?" "What is my preferred learning style?" "Can I give and receive feedback?" "Do I prefer to lead or to follow?" "What variables release my positive energy?" "Why should the company value me?" "What are my weaknesses?" "Where do I typically go for help?" Knowing yourself obviously contributes to job satisfaction. Defining areas of mismatch can be very helpful to corrective action that leads to higher performance.

5.11 Task Analysis: Administrative Issues

Description

This checklist suggests the most common issues faced by the performance consultant in the administration of a task analysis. It serves as a reminder to be thorough in your approach to task analysis.

Explanation

A *task* is the smallest essential element of a job. At the individual level, persons perform many tasks during a day, some with more expertise than others, some more willingly than others, some more happily than others, some in less time than others. The daily performance of job tasks is what people do at work. The quantity and quality of these tasks have an impact on an individual's performance. The relative importance, or weight, of tasks matters in terms of the assignment or investment of resources in them. Task analysis is an important part of analyzing individual performance.

This is the first of three tools dealing with task analysis.

What You Already Know That Can Help You

Technical trainers, technical instructional designers, and creators of software documentation manuals and *user guides* all know how important task analysis is to the successful learning of technical and procedural topics. The same detailed thoroughness of task analysis for training design is required for task analysis for performance analysis.

Task Analysis: Administrative Issues

Instructions: Refer to this checklist at the beginning of your design of task analysis.

____ 1. The result of a task analysis is a list of tasks for a specific job.

____ 2. A task has a beginning and an end. Define the beginning and end.

____ 3. Performance of a task can be measured. Define the measures.

____ 4. There are many ways to isolate the tasks required of a job. Examples are:

      a. Systematically observing someone doing them.
      b. Talking with experts.
      c. Analyzing a videotape of someone performing them.
      d. Checking work logs, equipment usage, error rates.
      e. Analyzing performance reviews.
      f. Analyzing productivity reports and work outputs.
      g. Analyzing the results of an employee survey requesting task information.

____ 5. Decide which task analysis procedure or procedures to follow.

____ 6. Design the task analysis data collection processes and instruments.

____ 7. Decide whether you will add the process of measuring performance on each task to the process of listing the tasks. If yes, plan carefully for the measurement activity after you have gotten verification of the task listing and the definition of the measures.

____ 8. Be prepared to allocate indices to the various tasks you name. Tools 5.12 and 5.13 give you guidance.

____ 9. Back up task analysis activities with administrative documentation: for example, a narrative description of analysis methods used, the person or persons doing the analysis, the date and time of the analysis, the job being broken down into tasks, the person in that job, the time that person has been in that job, a list of related jobs, etc. Differentiate this task analysis from all others: remember that this is *individual* performance analysis.

5.12 Task Analysis: Task Listings

Description

This form suggests a format for listing tasks, the first documentation activity in an individual performance analysis based on task analysis.

Explanation

The graphic on this page illustrates the relationship of task to job. In this graphic, the whole circle represents an occupation. Many jobs make up an occupation. Many duties and responsibilities make up jobs; these duties and responsibilities are further broken down into many tasks. An example illustrates the usefulness of task analysis. I shop at a supermarket where retarded adults have the job of bagging customers' groceries. My favorite bagger is Holly, a young woman with a million-dollar smile. From time to time, I watch Holly fulfill her responsibilities on the front line of customer service as she executes the tasks of her job. These are some of the tasks that Holly routinely does: make eye contact with and smile at the customer; take a bag from the pile and open it; place the bag on the loading shelf; start bagging when about half of the order is processed; put large cans and bottles on the bottom; put meats, fish, and poultry in plastic bags; put frozen foods in freezer bags; place produce where it won't get crushed; etc.

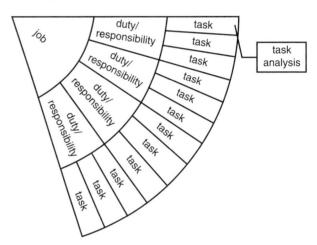

Source: Graphic adapted from Nilson, *Training Program Workbook & Kit* (Prentice Hall, 1989), p. 20.

Any of these tasks has performance qualities surrounding it: Does Holly need to practice establishing eye contact? Is it her responsibility to resupply the pile of empty bags? Does she know where supplies are kept? Is she capable of judging when the order has been about half processed or does she need a cue? Holly is a top performer; somebody has been paying attention to individual performance analysis in her case. Task analysis of her job and her unique characteristics are the foundation for performance excellence.

What You Already Know That Can Help You

Task analysis, with its resultant list of the many tasks that are characteristic of a job, has been a useful tool for *instructional designers* as they prepare *instructional materials* (instructional videos, electronic performance support systems, computer-based training, demonstrations, job aids, and ordinary instructor-led training). Technical trainers have been especially experienced in doing and making use of task analysis. Designers of robots and expert systems have also relied on task analysis as a basis of their work. Performance consultants who are on the trail of what makes good performance also find task analysis a useful tool.

Task Analysis: Task Listings

Instructions: Use a documentation form similar to this when you do your initial task analysis.

Task Listing

Person performing the tasks _____

Job title _____

Date of task listing _____ Time of the analysis _____

Name of task analyst _____

Method(s) of analysis _____

Note: Begin each task listing with an active verb. Add more pages if necessary.

1. _____	14. _____
2. _____	15. _____
3. _____	16. _____
4. _____	17. _____
5. _____	18. _____
6. _____	19. _____
7. _____	20. _____
8. _____	21. _____
9. _____	22. _____
10. _____	23. _____
11. _____	24. _____
12. _____	25. _____
13. _____	26. _____

5.13 Task Analysis: Task Groupings

Description

This chart contains examples of the many variables to consider when you further organize and categorize tasks to go one level deeper in task analysis.

Explanation

Several other levels of task analysis can lead to more accurate representation of a job, and ultimately help the person improve performance. These enhancements to a simple task listing are:

1. Grouping similar tasks, e.g., customer contact tasks, number-crunching tasks, communication tasks, etc.

2. Assigning an index to each task, e.g., a *difficulty* index of hard to perform, medium difficulty to perform, or easy to perform; a *value to the customer* index of high value, medium value, or low value; a *team-enabler* index of strong, neutral, or weak; a *frequency-per-hour* index; a *contributor-to-profit* index of great, moderate, or small.

3. Grouping tasks according to their cognitive demands or their contribution to the organization's competitive knowledge base.

4. Grouping tasks that seem related to an underlying competency, e.g., contributing to an ability to be objective, demonstrating a competency in planning, characterizing one as a good communicator, etc.

Grouping tasks can take you to many deeper analysis levels. It can also enhance your ability to accurately assess an individual's performance and eventually prescribe the most cost-effective interventions for improving individual performance.

What You Already Know That Can Help You

Trainers with a background in *measurement* relate to the value of indexing tasks. Instructional designers remember Bloom's and other educational psychologists' *taxonomies* and can understand the value of grouping similar items. Trainers with these kinds of experiences remember that training resources need to be applied and invested appropriately, targeted where the best learning can be expected to occur. This is not unlike determining where the best performance support resources need to be applied and invested. Going several directions deeper in your task analysis by indexing and grouping tasks is good for learning and for performance.

Task Analysis: Task Groupings

Instructions: Refer to this chart to help you decide the kinds of task groupings that are helpful to your client's performance. Use it to spark your imagination and develop variations of any of these ideas.

1. **Group similar tasks in categories.** Refer to your task listing (Tool 5.12), and reorganize the tasks into categories. Name the categories.

   Category _____   Category _____

   . _____   . _____

   . _____   . _____

   . _____   . _____

   Category _____   Category _____

   . _____   . _____

   . _____   . _____

   . _____   . _____

2. **Index each task** according to a meaningful index that ties in with your corporate mission, business unit, or personal goals. Create a documentation form to record your analysis according to each of the indices you specify.

		Tasks	*Index*				
			1	*2*	*3*	*4*	*5*
Index 1	difficulty (h, m, e)	1. _____					
Index 2	customer value (h, m, l)	2. _____					
Index 3	team enabler (s, n, w)	3. _____					
Index 4	frequency (use tic marks)	4. _____					
Index 5	contributor to profit (g, m, s)	5. _____					

3. **Group tasks according to their cognitive demand.** Each task can be coded according to the "smarts" it requires. For example, identifying the correct planning document is a lower-level cognitive skill than creating the contents of the plan. Planning has more cognitive demand than identifying. From your listing of tasks in Tool 5.12, index each task according to simple cognitive tasks, midlevel cognitive tasks, and complex cognitive tasks. This grouping can be very useful in establishing the nature of your client company's knowledge resource.

4. **Group tasks in relationship to competencies** that the company values. Companies responding to changes in technology, workforce diversity, and global competition are beginning to define the competencies they desire for their employees. An interesting exercise is to group tasks according to the "competencies for competitiveness" for the fast-arriving future. Competencies related to collaboration, personal initiative, knowledge creation, and evaluation are just some of the areas of competency being talked about today.

5.14 Individual Development Assessment

Description

This is a suggested format for an individual development assessment based on individual performance analysis.

Explanation

The Individual Development Assessment requires that the performance consultant synthesize findings from all analysis activities and relate them to the individual employee in a job. Tool 5.14 is meant to be a format suggestion; you will probably need to spread the information over several pages.

This is a reporting form, not yet a plan for action. It is meant to show employees how their jobs fit into the big picture of work at the company. The term "development" is used because of its connotation of more than just training or even learning. Development very easily could involve seeking organizational supports such as funding, rewards in another context, a rotational assignment, team membership, etc. as well as training for knowledge or skill building. Findings reported on this kind of form guide the employee and consultant to create, together, realistic action plans.

What You Already Know That Can Help You

Trainers and organizational development specialists recognize this as a form of feedback that should be governed by the classic rules of *giving and receiving feedback*. Any number of good resources are available today on 360-degree feedback, including a sizable number of your professional colleagues who have participated in such a process. Talk with them for tips about how to give feedback. See also Edwards and Ewen (1996) for numerous ideas about how to give feedback on performance, for format ideas for documentation and reporting forms, and for an appendix of more than 100 competencies on which performance analysis is often done.

Individual Development Assessment

Instructions: Use this as a guide for preparing feedback from your performance analysis activities to an individual. Focus on reporting; that is, remember that all feedback is good, whether it points out deficiencies or affirms excellence. This is still an analysis function; this form reports findings. These findings then lead to preparation of individual learning or development plans.

Job _____ Date _____

Employee's name _____

Performance analyst's name _____

Company's mission and its relationship to this job (narrative; several sentences):

_____

_____

_____

Competencies essential to this job (no more than seven):

_____

_____

_____

_____

_____

_____

_____

Variables of support for this job provided by the company (list):

_____

_____

_____

Effect of findings of job design analysis on this job (narrative):

_____

_____

_____

Findings of task analysis of this job (narrative or bullet list):

_____

_____

_____

Add pages or space to each item as needed; attach graphs or charts to further illustrate your findings.

173

Chapter 6

Diagnosing Performance Problems

Step 5: Determine standards, criteria, and performance objectives.

Step 6: Design and assemble diagnostic tools.

Step 7: Identify performance gaps.

This chapter deals with the various fundamental steps of diagnosing performance problems. Diagnosis is a more complicated process than analysis. It involves not breaking things down or apart into elements, as in analysis, but rather integrating and synthesizing—an exercise in seeing wholes rather than parts. Diagnosis brings together and attaches judgment. It involves making choices about importance, value, improvement, cause, possibility, and probability. Combining the strength of diagnosis with the notion of "performance problems" presents a powerful organizational process that can lead to improvements in both corporate and individual work life. The diagnosis of performance problems requires the performance consultant to review the many diverse findings of analysis activities previously done and to find patterns and structures, that is, to *synthesize* many separate elements into coherent entities. These entities are sometimes altogether new, and sometimes they are simply views of familiar elements presented from different perspectives and with enhanced dimensions.

This chapter begins with establishing a benchmark of goodness, that is, setting standards, criteria, and performance objectives against which ultimately to measure progress and success or failure. Diagnosis requires an understanding of goodness of fit and thereby a judgment about what should be. Design guidelines for the development of diagnostic tools are provided in this chapter, and examples are given. The chapter ends with a set of tools specifically included to help you identify performance gaps between what you've observed and analyzed as *present* reality and what you believe should be and could be performance in the *future*.

Nineteen tools are included in Chapter 6.

Tools in Chapter 6

STEP 5

**Step 5: Determine standards,
criteria,
and performance objectives.**
Use analysis information to determine
the reality of present standards,
the definition of many criteria
for excellence, and
the statement of specific
performance objectives.

6.1 Problem Definition and the Role of Standards

Description

This checklist contains ideas about what constitutes a problem, and it offers suggestions about the use of standards to help with diagnosis.

Explanation

Analysis activities yield a body of information that provides input to the task of diagnosing problems. Problem definition necessarily involves a real or implied standard, because without a standard you'd never know that you had a problem in the first place. Standards are grounded in current values about what defines a good or acceptable output of a work process. Standards allow employees to know that they are or aren't doing adequate work. Problems surface when standards are not met.

The reasons standards are not met can be many: Employees don't know what they are, that is, the standards haven't been communicated; there aren't any standards; there's no motivation to meet them; there's no evidence that anyone important cares about them; resources to support meeting standards are inadequate; equipment, tools, and processes are broken; standards are false, unrealistic, out of date, or unattainable; individuals don't have the skills to meet them; etc.

Analysis procedures point to potential sources of problems; problems get *diagnosed and defined* when the performance consultant makes a judgment about work based on standards that are apparent from analysis results. The art of diagnosis relies on your skills of synthesis, bringing together descriptive information and value judgment.

What You Already Know That Can Help You

Many business writers today speak eloquently about the postindustrial *age of the knowledge worker.* Indeed, knowledge seems to be the context of much of our work. Numerous voices are heard about how to structure and, above all, measure knowledge work and the business value of its unique outputs. One source of inspiration is Irish management consultant *Charles Handy* (1998) who suggests that the language of political theory, or how individuals and systems interact, has replaced the old engineering and property language of capital assets, labor costs, and balance sheets. In political theory, Handy says high-performing individuals prefer to be "led" by someone they respect instead of being considered property or resources with costs and liabilities attached to them. Handy suggests that "leadership, constituencies, alliances, power, and influence" are the components of politics, and these are much more descriptive of corporate life today than the notions of planning, control, and even management.

Other voices are those of *Robert S. Kaplan and David P. Norton* (1996). They argue forcefully for standards and measures other than financial ones, and suggest these three in addition: internal business processes, learning and growth, and the customer. Writers like these have a strong influence on how standards are defined.

Problem Definition and the Role of Standards

Instructions: Refer to this chart as you begin to diagnose and define problems from your assembled analysis information. Use these checklist items to spark your imagination; elaborate and add more items as you think of them. As you diagnose and define, write down the apparent standard associated with performance, keeping in mind that the standard represents reality (and often the minimum of acceptable performance). State the standard in words, attaching numbers where possible.

A. From analysis information, identify what work *values* characterize this company. Here are some possibilities:

___ 1. Getting close to the customer   ___ 5. Contributing to the knowledge base

___ 2. Creating higher margins   ___ 6. Seeking information

___ 3. Membership on a team   ___ 7. Making sales

___ 4. Individual visibility   ___ 8. Holding patents and copyrights

B. From analysis information, define worker *expectations* regarding:

___ 1. Their own personal contributions to company well-being.

___ 2. Amount and quality of company support for their own work.

___ 3. Their own involvement in satisfying customers.

___ 4. Career development opportunities.

___ 5. Pay, benefits, and perks.

___ 6. Visibility, appreciation, bonuses, rewards.

C. From analysis information, name and describe obvious *obstacles* to organizational and/or to individual performance.

1. _____   _____

2. _____   _____

3. _____   _____

Create a problem diagnosis documentation form to record your work. This is a start:

Values problems   Standard

_____   _____

_____   _____

_____   _____

Expectations problems   Standard

_____   _____

_____   _____

_____   _____

6.2 Chart of Likely Problem Sources

Description

This chart lists likely sources of problems and offers some insight into the synthesis tasks involved in problem diagnosis.

Explanation

This chart is designed to show you "synthesis thinking," that is, the kinds of mental operations you need to engage in to begin the diagnosis of performance problems. These are different mental skills from analysis skills, detailed in Chapter 5. Synthesis skills are those of bringing together and seeing relationships. Often the outcome of a synthesis is the construction of something altogether new—a new pattern, a new formula, a new system, a new point of view, a new awareness. In synthesis thinking, you pay attention to what gives life to the system and to what individuals value about their work. It is holistic rather than atomistic thinking, the forest rather than the trees, a focus on wholes first instead of parts first.

What You Already Know That Can Help You

Students of educational psychology will find background information in the work of Robert Gagne (1979), Florida State University; Benjamin Bloom (1956), University of Chicago; and Donald Norman (1993), University of California San Diego, among many others. A book by Richard A. Swanson, University of Minnesota, *Analysis for Improving Performance: Tools for Diagnosing Organizations and Documenting Workplace Expertise* (1994) is especially useful.

Chart of Likely Problem Sources

Instructions: Use this chart as a template for a diagnosis process. Of course, it could be much larger; what you see here is a sample of likely problem sources and synthesis responses that could be appropriate for each source. In its totality, it is meant to give you an idea of what's involved in using synthesis responses in problem diagnosis. For more sources of problems, see tools previously presented in this book: 2.3, 2.7, 2.9, 2.13, and 2.14.

Likely Problem Sources	*Synthesis Responses*
Knowledge or skills to do the job	– Discover similarities. – Construct a pattern of deficits. – Form a hypothesis.
Knowledge about the company and its customers	– Integrate customer complaints. – Discover implied expectations. – Isolate knowledge gaps. – Propose an information plan.
Incentives, rewards, consequences	– Derive relationships. – Point out inconsistencies. – Generate ideas for correction.
Expectations, standards, feedback	– Reformulate. – Integrate all measures. – Interpret the measurement system.
Money, support, help	– Discover a pattern. – Propose guidelines.
Internal work processes	– Derive relationships. – Construct patterns. – Change perspective.

6.3 The "Bridge" Matrix

Description

This 2×2 matrix is a bridge between the process of analysis and the process of diagnosis. It is a fundamental schematic illustrating four essential characteristics of performance consulting.

Explanation

Step 5 in the performance consulting process is "determine standards, criteria, and performance objectives." It changes direction, from analysis to diagnosis. It requires the addition of a value judgment or definition of "goodness" as standards are defined and play an important part in the continuation of the consulting process. Step 5 is the first step that focuses on the future and not on the past and present only. Diagnosing performance problems leads you forward because of the standards and value components.

This simple 2×2 matrix is a bridge between analysis and diagnosis, between what is and what should be, between actual and desirable. In the simple representation of the four cells of the matrix, you can see the fundamental structure of performance consulting.

What You Already Know That Can Help You

Trainers who have come from an *organizational development* background or who have been *management trainers* no doubt have used the 2×2 matrix in many ways. The "managerial grid" by Robert Blake and Jane Mouton, University of Texas, Austin (1964), was one of the earliest uses of the matrix to represent and explain organizational processes, and it has been widely used and adapted in studies of American workplaces over the decades since its first appearance. A later work by John Newstrom and Jon Pierce, University of Minnesota (1990), gives dozens of examples of effective use of the 2×2 matrix in management and organization studies.

The "Bridge" Matrix

Instructions: Refer to this graphic to see relationships in the performance consulting process as it relates to problem diagnosis. Use it as a template for your approach to consulting jobs.

Focus on the Present	Focus on the Future
ANALYSIS Description of the present situation	**DIAGNOSIS** Understanding that there is a problem based on standards
ANALYSIS Definition of cause(s)	**SYNTHESIS** Interrelationship of variables to desired improvement

6.4 Asking the Right Measurement Questions

Description

This checklist addresses the issue of designing measures of the performance consulting process.

Explanation

Diagnosing performance problems of necessity and by definition means that things get measured. Measurement, naturally, makes people nervous. People like to know that they "measure up" to their own and the company's expectations. People don't like to be minimized or made to look incompetent in front of their peers. It's an important early task of the performance consultant to calm the client's fears and insecurities about measurement, and to be disciplined about what to measure and how to conduct measurements.

The first three issues in Tool 6.4 must be addressed right away; engage in early dialogue with your client about them. These are the issues of intent, utility, and standards.

- *Intent:* It's tempting to count everything in sight and to bounce your resulting numbers against real or imagined standards of goodness. Take the time and objectivity to ask yourself the key question, "Why am I measuring this?" Ask the client to ask the same question. Probe for business reasons, for organizational or personal improvement reasons, for evidence that the intent is related to the company's mission. Agree with each other on the answers and then proceed to develop a measurement plan.

- *Utility:* Many people believe that the only significant measurement question is, "How will the results of measurement be used?" Collaborate with your client early in the performance consulting process to answer this key question. Measurement for its own sake gets you into a pile of trouble. Define clearly with your client how results will be used. Be sure that you see this definition within the parameters of your job as a performance consultant. Beware of hidden agendas and getting coopted in witch hunts. Relate the utility issue to organizational, structural, or functional decisions, such as customer relations, internal business processes, learning and knowledge development, or financial goals.

- *Standards:* When you are steeped in analysis activities, you naturally uncover information that begins to suggest standards. As you synthesize analysis information and problems start to become obvious, you're tempted to jump to conclusions about standards—their presence or their absence, their wrongheadedness, their relevance, and a host of other assumptions. Take it easy, and ask of your data the "reasonableness" question. You have in front of you mountains of data from analysis and synthesis activities; you need to temper the complexity of what you've done with the simple question, "Is this a reasonable standard, given what I see before me?" Only when you've answered that to your satisfaction and your client's can you define the standards.

What You Already Know That Can Help You

A simple admonition: Look before you leap; and think, "were in this together."

Asking the Right Measurement Questions

Instructions: Use this checklist of key questions to focus your attention on the issues involved in dealing with the variables of the up-front or beginning processes of measurement.

Issues	Key Questions
Intent	1. Why am I measuring this?
Utility	2. How will the results of measurement be used?
Standards	3. Do standards exist? Are they reasonable? What are they?
Focus	4. What variables do I need to measure?
Resources	5. Can I get the information I need to develop criteria and performance objectives?
Support	6. Will existing measurement systems and tools work for me?
New work	7. Do I need to develop new standards, measures, tools?
Procedures	8. What specific procedures do I need to follow?
Staffing	9. Who should do the measuring?
Feedback	10. Who should be involved in feedback of results?
Obstacles	11. What are the possible obstacles to valid measurement?
Timeline	12. What timeline do I need to follow?

6.5 Setting Criteria for What Should Be

Description

This chart focuses on criteria, what they are, and how to express them to work toward the desired future.

Explanation

When you have determined through analysis and synthesis activities that performance problems exist, you must establish goals or targets for solving the problems. You have to set up a structure for getting from where you are to where you want to be. The first part of this structuring is the process of establishing criteria.

If an individual, a process, or even a large system is not measuring up to the company's work standard, you now have the challenge of specifying exactly what must be done to either meet the existing standard or to define a different standard. You need to get answers. How much? What quantity of? Does this or that criterion represent excellent performance? You need to target areas of improvement, groupings of job tasks or clusters of processes or parts of systems that need special attention to arrive at "what should be."

We talk about criteria as groupings: skill sets, criteria areas, elements of a larger entity, benchmarks. We think of criteria in the plural, that is, *sets* of components that, if addressed with discipline and vigor, point the way from where we are to where we want to be. Criteria come from everywhere: policies, organization structures, issues of morale, procedures, reporting relationships, leadership styles, opportunities for growth and personal development, job definitions, etc. Defining them requires divergent thinking, innovative ways of seeing wholes in parts, creative ways of grouping ideas and work functions together.

Criteria are not plans; they are targets. They make sense because of the confluence of future-focused elements that can improve performance—measurable improvements that you and your client see as "what should be."

What You Already Know That Can Help You

The business press is full of evidence that criteria-setting is an important job for all kinds of employees and all kinds of situations. Trainers who read widely recognize criteria in many sources. Some from the recent *business press and professional training publications* are by Patterson (1996, p. 58), Matson (1998, p. 196), and the Center for Creative Leadership (1998, p. 8).

Setting Criteria for What Should Be

Instructions: Refer to this chart as a quick view of setting criteria. The top band is the broadest; each lower band becomes more specific.

1. **STANDARD:** Focused on the present or past.

2. **CRITERIA:** Focused on the future.
"What Should Be?"

3. **CRITERIA:** A set of desired outcomes
to encourage and guide change;
requires innovative thinking,
scanning the whole company.

4. **CRITERIA:** Need measures of performance
to establish what's
considered mastery of them—
ways to know what you know.

5. **QUALITATIVE CRITERIA STATEMENTS:**
Need to be turned into
quantitative elements
so that they can be measured
(percents, dollars, frequencies,
sums, differences, etc.).

6.6 The Baldrige Criteria

Description

This most famous set of criteria is included here as an illustration of the value and use of criteria. The 1998 criteria are featured from The Malcolm Baldrige National Quality Award *Criteria for Performance Excellence* booklet.

Explanation

Twenty items in seven categories provide organizations with an integrated, results-oriented framework for implementing and assessing processes for managing all operations. These *Criteria for Performance Excellence* are also the basis for giving Baldrige National Quality Awards and providing feedback to applicants. The 1998 booklet makes it very clear that the award is given for results, not for specific products or services. A cover letter with the booklet states that the 1998 criteria:

> *further strengthen the systems view of performance management and place a greater emphasis on the alignment of company strategy, customer and market knowledge, a high performance work force, key company processes, and business results. Increased focus has been given to all aspects of organizational and employee learning.* [December 1997 letter from Harry S. Hertz, Director]

Scoring guidelines are provided in the *Criteria* booklet; these spell out the assessment dimensions—Approach, Deployment, and Results—and the key factors used to assess against each dimension (p. 44). Here's a list of the 20 items, with their point value (of a total of 1,000 points); seven categories are on Tool 6.6:

1.1 Leadership System (80)

1.2 Company Responsibility and Citizenship (30)

2.1 Strategy Development Process (40)
2.2 Company Strategy (40)

3.1 Customer and Market Knowledge (40)
3.2 Customer Satisfaction and Relationship Enhancement (40)
4.1 Selection and Use of Information and Data (25)
4.2 Selection and Use of Comparative Information and Data (15)

4.3 Analysis and Review of Company Performance (40)
5.1 Work Systems (40)
5.2 Employee Education, Training, & Development (30)
5.3 Employee Well-Being and Satisfaction (30)
6.1 Management of Product & Service Processes (60)
6.2 Management of Support Processes (20)
6.3 Management of Supplier and Partnering Processes (20)
7.1 Customer Satisfaction Results (125)
7.2 Financial and Market Results (125)
7.3 Human Resource Results (50)
7.4 Supplier and Partner Results (25)
7.5 Company-Specific Results (125)

What You Already Know That Can Help You

The Malcolm Baldrige National Quality Award was created by public law in 1987. Award criteria booklets from that date through 1996 were entitled simply that. In 1997, however, the focus changed and the title of the booklet became what it is today, *Criteria for **Performance** Excellence* (boldface mine). Trainers who have been around for any of these years no doubt have been involved somehow in *The Baldrige*. What's important now is that the focus has changed to *performance* and trainers must shift focus too. Get more information from the American Society for Quality (ASQ), Milwaukee, WI, 800/248-1946, or from the National Quality Program office at the National Institute of Standards and Technology (Department of Commerce), Gaithersburg, MD, 301/975-2036.

The Baldrige Criteria

Instructions: Refer to this chart to study how these criteria are grouped to lead to "performance excellence" or to lead your organization forward to request more information about "The Baldrige" from ASQ or the Department of Commerce. A 1000 points represents 100%; the numerator indicates the point value for each category.

1. **Leadership:** The company's leadership system, values, expectations, and public responsibilities. — **110/1000**

2. **Strategic Planning:** The effectiveness of strategic and business planning and deployment of plans, with a strong focus on customer and operational performance requirements. — **80/1000**

3. **Customer and Market Focus:** How the company determines customer and market requirements and expectations, enhances relationships with customers, and determines their satisfaction. — **80/1000**

4. **Information and Analysis:** The effectiveness of information collection and analysis to support customer-driven performance excellence and marketplace success. — **80/1000**

5. **Human Resource Focus:** The success of efforts to realize the full potential of the work force to create a high-performance organization. — **100/1000**

6. **Process Management:** The effectiveness of systems and processes for assuring the quality of products and services. — **100/1000**

7. **Business Results:** Performance results, trends, and comparison to competitors in key business areas—customer satisfaction, financial and marketplace, human resources, suppliers and partners, and operations. — **450/1000**

Source: From *The 1998 Criteria for Performance Excellence*, p. 2, and *1998 Application Forms and Instructions, p. 2.*

6.7 Criteria versus Norms

Description

This chart differentiates between criteria and norms, the two most often used perspectives on measurement.

Explanation

One reason why trainers have trouble understanding criteria is that most of our experience with measurement has been with *norm-referenced* testing. In schools and colleges, we were given quizzes, tests on units of instruction, and final exams that assessed our standing in the group of our classmates who also took the same tests. Results of the assessment (the test) were *normed,* that is, displayed in a normal curve, a bell-shaped graph that more often than not showed only a few outstandingly good individuals (scores) at the head of the class (the right tail of the normal curve) and a corresponding few outstandingly bad individuals (scores) at the bottom of the class (the left tail of the normal curve). Most scores, of course, fell in the middle 68% of the bell. Learning for most of us has been interpreted by norm-referenced assessments. We are accustomed to being compared with our fellow test takers at report card time, when we take SATs to get into college, and when we take GMATs to get into graduate schools. We are used to having acceptable "performance" set by group comparison.

This is not what criterion-referenced assessment is all about, however. When we set a criterion, we commit to measurement against a standard of performance for that content only, not against a group of other persons. Our criterion score represents performance against a definition of specific skills or knowledge desirable for that item. What counts in the workplace is the measurable quality and added value that individuals bring to their jobs—an indication of performance against well-defined criteria. Our workplaces are much too complex, and our jobs are too individualistic, to choose norm-referenced assessments to yield useful scores for *performance improvement.* Criterion-referenced assessments are a much more practical choice.

What You Already Know That Can Help You

Most of *safety training and testing* has been criterion-referenced, as has *assessment* for *technical training for manufacturing and for operating computers. Assessment of sales training* techniques has also frequently been criterion-referenced. It's somewhat of a stretch for many trainers to think of criterion assessment development and implementation techniques in relation to organizational performance. Yet that's precisely the change in measurement perspective necessary when you diagnose performance problems.

Criteria versus Norms

Instructions: Refer to this chart for a quick and easy refresher about measurement before you design measurement instruments and surveys or information-gathering plans.

CRITERION-REFERENCED ASSESSMENT

Example: Four nuts attach the axle to the wheel rim of your car and they all have to be tightened when fixing a flat tire. When your friend helped you out by fixing your flat, he forgot to tighten one of the nuts. Four nuts = performing to 100% of the criterion. Your friend's assessment was therefore 75%. His score is useful in showing where he can improve his performance.

NORM-REFERENCED ASSESSMENT

Example: A typing speed test is given to all entry-level word processing operators. Fifty individuals took the test. 100 different measurements were made. The average score was 82 out of 100. Your score was 90, or less than 10% above the average. You are placed on the normal curve a little to the right of the center of the bell curve. Since the norm was high, your score of 90 isn't that outstanding. In fact, a score of 90 could be demotivating for you; seeing yourself near the center of the bell doesn't give you very much useful information to make improvements in your performance.

6.8 Establishing Performance Objectives

Description

This chart presents a format for establishing performance objectives.

Explanation

Assessment planning—that is, the design of measurement—now begins in earnest with the establishment of performance objectives for each of the items in your criteria list. The chart in Tool 6.8 suggests a "formula" for creating measurable objectives. This formula is based on the landmark work of Mager (1975). Simply stated, it is:

Do this, to this, in this amount, under these conditions.

When companies decide to apply for The Baldrige National Quality Award, for example, they develop their own measurable performance objectives in each of the seven categories prescribed by The Baldrige Criteria (see Tool 6.6). They then measure themselves according to their own performance objectives, and when they're satisfied that they measure up, they submit their applications. If they find that they don't measure up to their own performance objectives, they make improvements so that they can perform at 100% of their definitions of excellence. Then they submit their applications to The Baldrige. Performance objectives refer to, and are grounded in, a company's own unique definitions of excellence. Criterion-referenced assessment is what matters to the Department of Commerce, National Institute of Standards and Technology, which administers The Baldridge.

What You Already Know That Can Help You

Technical trainers have grown up with *behavioral objectives*. Early in the development of the science of instructional design, several major battles were fought and won. The first was between the thinkers and the doers, and the doers won. Learning was seen to be rooted in experience. Observable behavioral change was the goal of measurement. The second was between perspectives, that of the teacher or that of the student, and the student won. Objectives for learning were to be stated not in terms of what the instructor would teach, but rather what the student would learn. These two bases of the field persist and are reflected in such movements as the situated cognition perspective, embedded performance support systems, and communities of practice. The move of training to performance is part of the evolution of the field, especially obvious in instructional design. Trainers who know and love behavioral objectives are comfortable dealing with performance objectives. The focus now becomes organizational, rather than just individual; all that goes into performance rather than just the design of instructional details.

Establishing Performance Objectives

Instructions: Use this chart ultimately to design measurements. For each item in your list of criteria for excellent performance, develop a performance objective—a specific quantifiable target that's representative of your company's unique strengths and requirements of success. Focus on what persons, processes, or organizations have to do to be considered top performers.

Do This:	To This:	In This Amount:	Under These Conditions:
Use an active verb. 1	The object/person that will benefit from high performance 2	A measurable numerical target 3	When? Where? How? 4

Examples of performance objectives:

• (**Person**)   *Increase*   *customer service visits*   *by 10% per week*   *on B list accounts.*
              1   2   3   4

• (**Process**)   *Show a downward slope*   *to classroom training registration numbers* by
                           1   2

              at least 6 degrees   *for the next three training starts in April, May, and June.*
                      3   4

• (**Organization**)   *Build*   *profit margin*   *from its current 12% to 16%* by
                            1   2   3

              November 30.
                    4

STEP 6

**Step 6: Design and assemble
diagnostic tools.**
Design a measurement system
and diagnostic tools within it.
Be guided by criteria you have set
and by your specific and unique
performance objectives.

6.9 Planning Strategy for Performance Diagnosis

Description

This combination checklist and chart indicates ways to keep yourself organized as you do the work of performance diagnosis.

Explanation

The process of engaging in performance diagnosis can be complicated, time-consuming, resource-rich, and marred by misunderstandings. You need to do everything in your power to expedite this process, guarantee its fairness, and make it a learning opportunity for all involved.

One of the ways you can do this is to have a clear strategy before you begin. Tool 6.9 can help you see what you need to do in terms of planning.

What You Already Know That Can Help You

Planning for performance diagnosis is like *any other business process*. It has time, money, learning, and people dimensions. It is served well by careful planning and documentation. Trainers probably have had some experience in budget planning, curriculum planning, public relations planning, team planning, information system planning. All these planning processes are similar to planning for performance diagnosis.

Planning Strategy for Performance Diagnosis

Instructions: Refer to this tool before you devise a plan for engaging in performance diagnosis. It is a template only; add pages to sections as necessary.

___ What kinds of forms do you need for this particular diagnosis?
___ Do you need to create new evaluation forms? ___ New administration forms?
___ Did you do a thorough analysis of which individuals need to know about this?
___ Are various sites for observation or data collection involved? ___ Travel required?
___ Do you need field testing or hypothesis testing of new or untried instruments?
___ Do you need a budget for this performance diagnosis?
___ Do you need statistical analysis services or scoring services? ___ Who? ___ Cost?
___ Do you have a plan for sharing your findings and for giving feedback?
___ How and when will you present conclusions and recommendations to your client?

Performance objective _____

_____

Business goal directly addressed by this diagnosis process _____

_____

Timeline for measuring this objective _____

Person who will be lead evaluator _____

Sources of relevant information:

Documents	*People*
_____	_____
_____	_____
_____	_____

Look for these indicators in all investigations _____

_____

_____

Best procedures to follow _____

_____

_____

Findings: _____

Conclusions: _____

Recommendations: _____

_____

_____

6.10 Aligning Criteria with Business Goals

Description

This chart suggests a format in which performance criteria can be represented in alignment with business goals.

Explanation

There are two important ideas in the literature about high-performance workplaces. One is *synergy,* meaning a working together of the systems, processes, and people that make up a company. The other is *alignment,* which is a conscious maneuvering and matching up of aspirations, motivations, and plans across workplace structures, levels, and positions. One source of these ideas is Bassi and Van Buren (1997, pp. 32–41). Another source is Senge and Kleiner (1994, pp. 297–347). Sources such as these suggest that high-performing and learning organizations pay a great deal of attention to creating and nurturing synergy and to aligning performance improvement opportunities and processes with their stated business goals. Senge even goes so far as to say near the beginning of his chapter on shared vision that "every organization has a destiny" and that the challenge in developing shared vision is to converse and listen for the expression of that destiny so that the organization becomes creative (p. 298).

As the performance consultant beginning to diagnose performance problems, you and your client can design tools to address issues of goal alignment as you use your criteria to move forward into performance improvement.

What You Already Know That Can Help You

Trainers who have been involved in *team training* have become familiar with ideas like synergy and alignment, and with the importance of process as well as content. In the case of performance improvement, you are dealing with assessment and measurement processes in addition to building organizations. In measurement especially, it's important to document relationships.

Aligning Criteria with Business Goals

Instructions: Refer to this chart for ideas about how to represent the performance-diagnosis process so that it moves the company toward its expressed goals. Construct your own chart or schematic to illustrate features and system relationships that you believe are important in the company.

Goal Alignment

This alignment process enables every organization and employees at every level to see how the overarching business goals are reflected or contained within the business goals of departments and other business units. In this process, criteria for performance improvement are grouped in relationship to both the "big picture" business goal and the "smaller picture" department or unit goal.

Goal Alignment

Statement of corporate business goal _____

_____

Business unit goal related to this corporate business goal _____

_____

Criteria that lead toward these goals

- _____
- _____
- _____
- _____

Action plan for diagnosis activities, assessments, and evaluations _____

_____

_____

_____

_____

6.11 Administration and Project Management

Description

This chart suggests a format for treating performance diagnosis as a project. Project management basics are represented.

Explanation

Tool 6.11 is a project administration and accountability form. It is especially appropriate for performance-diagnosis processes that, in the client's view, must be related to larger business goals. The outcome of performance-diagnosis activities, of course, is identification of problems. Both consultant and client deserve to know that diagnostic activities and evaluation activities are appropriate, fair, managed carefully, fiscally responsible, and cost-effective. Both consultant and client need to have a tangible reference document to guide future work. Tool 6.11 is this kind of document.

What You Already Know That Can Help You

Consulting work is quite different from training in its accountability structures. Training work is often governed by a master schedule—needs assessment time, instructional design time, time for development of course materials, pilot testing of new courses, and final delivery of sessions of the course. All these are built into a schedule that is more or less predictable. Accountability in training work depends on the trainer's ability to meet the schedule targets and deliver materials required for the next phase of the process. The trainer's accountability with students more often than not depends on an end-of-course "smiles sheet" evaluation, which generally has no relationship to the trainer's pay or to corporate business goals. Accountability in training has typically stayed within the training loop, seldom breaking out into the larger corporate loop.

Training has tended to stay stuck in its own bureaucracy. Training, of course, has been criticized for this insularity. A popular workshop at national training and human resources conferences in recent years has been the workshop on *Return on Investment (ROI) in training,* and other similar sounding workshops that offer ways to make training more accountable in terms of the company's business goals. Study after study has shown that very few training departments have the interest, time, or skills to evaluate the financial impact of training on business goals (Kirkpatrick's "Level 4" evaluation). Jack Phillips and Don Kirkpatrick are two *training* authors currently speaking and writing on the subject.

Consulting work, on the other hand, is more entrepreneurial. Its accountability structures are always in the forefront. Clients are always watching to be sure you are not wasting time and money; you are always driven to deliver value in the most reasonable amount of time. Consulting work is often seen as "project work," governed by project management accountability ideas and procedures.

Administration and Project Management

Instructions: Review this chart for ideas about managing performance diagnosis as a project. Create your own documentation forms to guide your work and keep it accountable to your client's interests.

One of the best ways to remain accountable, as well as to help yourself always keep "the big picture" in mind as you are mired in the details of performance diagnosis, is to keep a project notebook, a three-ring binder of management functions you are contracted to fulfill. Make four tabs:

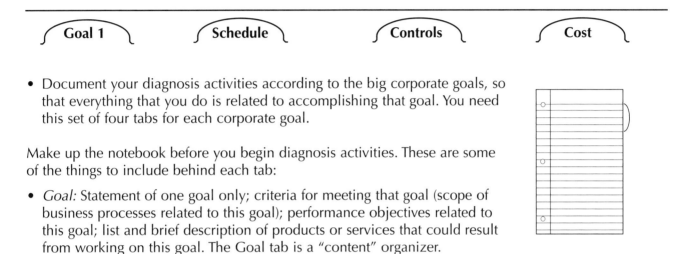

- Document your diagnosis activities according to the big corporate goals, so that everything that you do is related to accomplishing that goal. You need this set of four tabs for each corporate goal.

Make up the notebook before you begin diagnosis activities. These are some of the things to include behind each tab:

- *Goal:* Statement of one goal only; criteria for meeting that goal (scope of business processes related to this goal); performance objectives related to this goal; list and brief description of products or services that could result from working on this goal. The Goal tab is a "content" organizer.

- *Schedule:* Milestones for completing work, expressed as a Gantt chart timeline or as a timeline with activity points or tasks in list form under key dates; a chart listing person-days expended on a daily basis on this goal. The Schedule tab should contain a planning document as well as a daily log—for this goal only.

- *Controls:* Maps and graphics indicating person-to-person relationships, roles, and responsibilities; correspondence generated and received; file copies of your weekly status report of what you accomplished, what is still pending, and what you perceive as modifications needed; documentation and reports of in-process reviews and other evaluation results documents. The Controls tab contains everything pertaining to what you actually did and who was involved, and it contains lots of narrative—lots of words about work done.

- *Cost:* Pay expressed as person-days; materials cost; travel cost; cost of purchased services such as auditing, art and graphics, printing and binding.

203

6.12 Tool Options for Individual Performance Diagnosis

Description

This chart lists common types of diagnostic tools, with key issues regarding the use of each for individual performance diagnosis.

Explanation

Individual performance diagnosis must first be concerned with fairness, privacy, and issues of civil rights, not only with employment opportunities. There are many options for choosing the right tool or tools to do a comprehensive and efficient individual performance diagnosis. However, you should thoughtfully consider the issues involved in designing, administering, scoring, and using the results of the various tool options before you develop your plan for interacting with individuals. Tool 6.12 gets you thinking about all these issues.

What You Already Know That Will Help You

Trainers who have come from a sales and *marketing background* or with experience in *educational research* are familiar with a variety of "tools" that are useful with individuals: consumer surveys, survey research for a master's degree or doctoral research, market studies of all sorts, reports of study results in academic journals. All these have familiar documentation structures that are similar to the tool options presented here. Trainers-turned-performance-consultants would do well to refer to design sources in these other fields for help in the design of instruments for use with individuals.

Tool Options for Individual Performance Diagnosis

Instructions: Refer to this chart for ideas regarding the design and use of diagnostic tools for individual performance diagnosis.

1. *Questionnaire/survey:* Useful in self-reporting of strengths and weaknesses based on knowledge and skills. Easy-to-score/tally results if "closed questions" are used (questions with unequivocal responses). Useful also in personnel rating such as in 360-degree evaluations. Useful in measuring opinions and attitudes based on self-reporting. Time-consuming to construct valid and reliable instruments with appropriate scales; waiting period to get results. Easy to administer on a PC.

2. *Interview:* Useful when face-to-face communication is important to the responder's comfort. Can be a helpful trust-building tool. Interview questions (the "interview schedule") must be carefully designed around core competencies, stated business goals, or specific performance problems in order to elicit in-depth responses. This tool requires a trained and skillful interviewer who knows when to ask the responder to "say more." Can turn into a gripe session unless structure and discipline, with kindness, are maintained during interviewing. Choice of recording method is necessary, and permission must be granted by the responder ahead of the interview (tape recording, video recording, scribe).

3. *Observation:* Useful for structured job and task problem diagnosis. Requires prior consensus from the subject of the observation that tasks to be observed are nontrivial and related to business goals. Like the interview, is labor-intensive and one-on-one, and must be carefully designed especially around the issue of validity.

4. *Narrative:* Useful when context is important to the diagnosis. Useful for describing relationships—individuals to systems, how procedures work, people to people. Important when you are looking for patterns. Use "open questions" to encourage free response. Consider these typical narrative tools: reports of critical incidents, scenario development and comparison, case study, keeping a journal. Fairly easy to design and administer; difficult to interpret. Usefulness increases with active feedback and follow-up dialogue with the responder.

5. *Cue card:* Useful with individuals whose quality of response can benefit from cues. Useful in helping individuals zero in on performance elements "in the background," which they might not be able to readily identify or articulate. Difficult to design; easy to administer. Game-like and fun. Results can be extremely useful in categorizing problem areas for targets of improvement efforts. See Tool 6.15 for more information.

6. *Document review:* Useful in determining problem context. Requires sensitivity to an individual's right to privacy; sometimes difficult to gain access to documents you need for a valid investigation. Can save time and yield a "broad brush" picture of the individual's work environment. A supplement to the other tools.

6.13 Tool Options for Process Performance Diagnosis

Description

This chart lists common types of diagnostic tools, with key issues regarding use of each for diagnosis of process performance.

Explanation

The diagnosis of process performance deals with the variables apparent in making a business process work. Categories of some common processes are those associated with manufacturing, with sales, with information collection and distribution, with engineering, with empowerment, communication, learning. Performance consultants are very often called in to diagnose process problems originating in any of these common categories. Work processes obviously affect individual performance, and are indicators of organizational health. In short, processes stand in the middle of both ends of the range of workplace performance.

What You Already Know That Can Help You

Trainers who have had experience in the total quality management (*TQM*) movement and/or in *team building,* workplace *diversity,* and *empowerment* relate to the importance of process. Instructional designers who have labored long and hard to create courses and instructional experiences know the necessity of paying attention to the design of process, just as much as design of content, for learning to occur. The *process versus content* argument has been with trainers for a long time. These understandings can help you as you diagnose process performance in your client company. Good information about process quality is available from the American Society for Quality (ASQ), Milwaukee, WI, 800/248-1946. Phone them for a current publications list. The ASTD *Infoline* collection of tool booklets can also be a good source of ideas. Phone the American Society for Training and Development (ASTD) at 800/628-2783 for a current catalog of *Infolines.*

Tool Options for Process Performance Diagnosis

Instructions: Refer to this chart for ideas regarding the design and use of diagnostic tools for diagnosis of process performance.

1. *Questionnaire/survey:* Useful in gathering employees' opinions about process—how a process works or doesn't work, what are the results of the process, what are obstacles, etc. Results of questionnaires are easy to report and disseminate.

2. *Interview:* Could be too time-consuming because you want answers from a large number of respondents to validate the reliability of the process; you want to be sure that the answers you get accurately describe the way the process works across a broad spectrum of respondents. Interviewing a large number of individuals to get a sense of reliability that the process behaves similarly in many situations simply takes too much time. Useful if you need clarification *after* use of a broad-scale instrument; then sampling the respondent population for interviews might be an approach to save time and still use the Interview as a diagnostic technique.

3. *Observation:* Useful in describing the design of a process and its system relationships. Useful also in determining consequences of the process, either as strengths or as weaknesses. Develop a good observation checklist ahead of time.

4. *Narrative:* Narrative techniques of critical incident reporting and journal keeping are especially useful for diagnosing process performance. Those persons involved in the effects of the process are the best ones to say exactly how the process performs. Such narrative accounts can be gathered from many persons and compared by the consultant for a good picture of the process. Be sure to give respondents a few key words on which to organize their critical incident documentation and tell them what to observe prior to writing in their journals.

5. *Cue card:* Useful in providing a thorough description of a process. Difficult to design a "necessary and sufficient" cue card for each process, but fun to try. Useful for wide distribution because it is easy to administer and tally.

6. *Document review:* Useful to catalog the results of processes. Can provide context outside the process itself, which can be useful in establishing important business relationships between and among processes. A danger in selection—that is, you need to be sure that the documents you choose provide a complete picture so that your conclusions are not biased or incomplete.

6.14 Tool Options for Organizational Performance Diagnosis

Description

This chart lists common types of diagnostic tools, with key issues regarding the use of each for organizational performance diagnosis.

Explanation

Recall the earlier discussion about corporate mission statements, corporate values and culture, and finding better ways to standardize corporate performance other than financial performance (for example, see Tool 6.1 or Tool 5.5). Diagnosing organizational performance requires that you see the "big picture" of organizational performance as it represents the whole of individual and process performance. Diagnosing organizational performance is a tougher job than diagnosing either individual or process performance simply because the two basic tests of measurement are more difficult to pass. Designing valid and reliable measures of something so large and complex as an organization is difficult, as is including only what is necessary but all that's sufficient in your diagnosis plan.

Before you begin an organizational diagnosis, do as Kaplan and Norton (1996) did and determine three or four standards for organizational performance that reflect your company's goals and mission. Develop stretch criteria and organizational performance objectives within each of these standards. Segment and focus your diagnosis tools, so that meaningful and useful results are obtained. Clarify what it means to learn as an organization, and index your diagnostic findings to organizational learning factors.

What You Already Know That Can Help You

Training literature during the 1990s has been full of *organizational learning*. A familiar source within this literature base is Victoria Marsick of Columbia University and her collaborator, Karen Watkins, University of Georgia (1992). Their work is specifically directed to trainers who need to think more broadly and more organizationally. Look up their references in your libraries or online. Also review Kaplan and Norton's work, which is more technical and more focused on measures of organizational "goodness" in today's knowledge-based companies. Another look at the pioneering work of Tom Gilbert (1978) can refresh your memory about the "environmental supports," what the organization provides for performance. These together can give you a good feel for what needs to be done in terms of organizational performance diagnosis.

Tool Options for Organizational Performance Diagnosis

Instructions: Refer to this chart for ideas regarding the design and use of diagnostic tools for diagnosis of organizational performance.

1. *Questionnaire/survey:* Useful as a means to solicit input from everyone in an organization. Easy to administer, tally, and report feedback. Time-consuming to design because of the complexity of organizations; items should probably be categorized according to areas such as "operations," "customer service," "employee development," "competitive positioning," "worklife quality," etc. to help respondents keep their thinking focused on one area at a time. Results are more useful if they are unconfounded; careful questionnaire design can foster better results.

2. *Interview:* Time-consuming but useful for a sample of respondents; for example, a sample of customers, suppliers, board members, front-line supervisors, city politicians. Useful when the interviewer's role can help draw out responses. Useful when respondents might require clarification.

3. *Observation:* Probably not useful for organizational performance diagnosis. However, a diagnostic activity could be designed around observation of a process. Take, for example, order fulfillment: The consultant could figuratively "ride piggyback on the order" and track it from the time it was placed to the time it was fulfilled, noting all the organizational influences on it. In such an observation, the results would be helped if more than one observer were used, yielding a multirater evaluation.

4. *Narrative:* Probably best used in conjunction with the questionnaire, as an item on the survey form. Could also be useful with a group, persons holding a job title, or team. Hard to interpret and score; time-consuming.

5. *Cue card:* Probably not useful in organizational performance diagnosis because there are too many variables and design of the instrument is difficult. A danger that the structuring of the cue card would be limiting rather than expansive. Could stifle rather than encourage creative thinking.

6. *Document review:* Useful as a source of quantitative information: how many, how much, when, how long, etc.? Be sure to have a plan for seeking information from documents; that is, organize your thinking into the categories you need or around the specific organizational performance objectives you have identified. An important source of organizational performance information, but should be complemented by the input of individuals through other techniques such as questionnaires, interviews, observations, and narrative statements.

6.15 Scales and Rating Systems

Description

This chart illustrates common scales, rating systems, and schematics that are typically used in the measurement and reporting of results.

Explanation

People are aided in their diagnostic abilities by graphic devices that represent or illustrate their thinking. Each of these graphics approaches diagnosis from a different angle. These are some of the key points about each:

- *Scales:* Always keep the logic the same; present all scales used in the same diagnosis effort so that they "read" the same way—low to high, minus to plus, etc. Be sure that scales are calibrated evenly and equally, so that each interval is of equal weight or value. Most people prefer scales of no more than 10 and no fewer than 3 choices. Using an even number (e.g., 4, 6) of choice points prevents a responder from always choosing the middle. Scales are usually presented as a line, but can also be presented matrix-style with choices marked by checkmarks in matrix cells.

- *Cue card:* The cue card is a chart of probable choices, organized into boxes that represent criteria, other organizational entities, or work or worker characteristics. This system of choosing aims to help the respondent differentiate among probable choices, and helps a person narrow and more carefully define response. The respondent is asked to simply circle the *one best* descriptor. Here are two examples:

A. *Incentives*	**B.** *Information*
Infrequent	Inaccessible
Trivial	Unclear
Nonexistent	Incomplete
Poorly timed	Insufficient
Irrelevant	Untimely

- *Radar chart:* This system rating graphic is detailed in a book by *Fortune* magazine writer, Thomas A. Stewart (1997, pp. 244ff). To construct a radar chart, the respondent registers votes on each axis, calibrated from zero at the center of the circle to, for example, 10 at the outer rim. Each axis represents a different criterion (see, for example, The Baldrige Criteria, Tool 6.6). More axes can be specified. After addressing all axes, draw a line connecting the points. The polygon resulting from the center outward represents what you have; shade or stipple this to make it stand out. The remaining white space toward the outside of the circle represents what you want.

- *Ishikawa Fishbone chart:* Although developed for manufacturing applications, this cause-and-effect chart can be adapted to performance consulting, which also recognizes the importance of influences other than just skills and knowledge.

What You Already Know That Can Help You

Review the tools you've used or heard about from the *quality movement*. Adapt them as necessary. Don't be afraid to design and assemble all tools that seem appropriate.

Scales and Rating Systems

Instructions: Study these four different types of representations as you decide on what kinds of diagnostic tools you will use in your performance diagnoses.

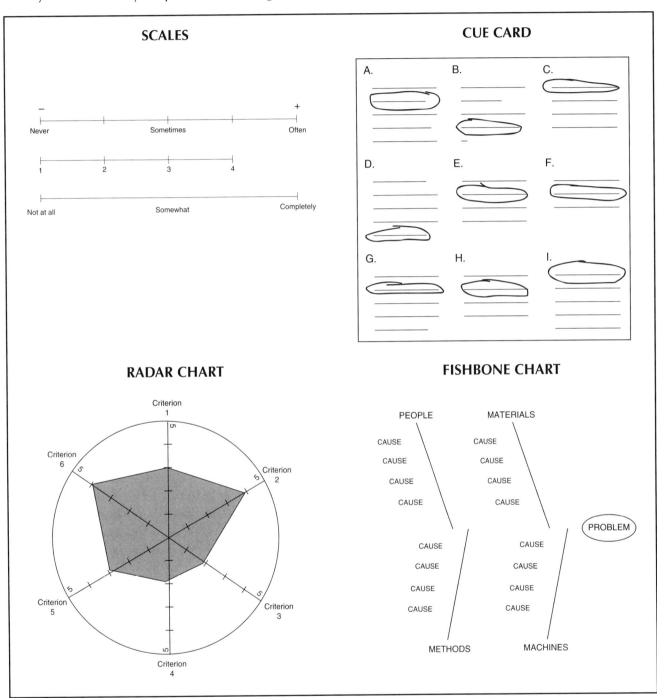

SCALES

Never   Sometimes   Often

1   2   3   4

Not at all   Somewhat   Completely

CUE CARD

A. B. C. D. E. F. G. H. I.

RADAR CHART

Criterion 1
Criterion 2
Criterion 3
Criterion 4
Criterion 5
Criterion 6

FISHBONE CHART

PEOPLE   MATERIALS
CAUSE   CAUSE
CAUSE   CAUSE
CAUSE   CAUSE
CAUSE   CAUSE
PROBLEM
CAUSE   CAUSE
CAUSE   CAUSE
CAUSE   CAUSE
CAUSE   CAUSE
METHODS   MACHINES

STEP 7

Step 7: Identify performance gaps.
Using all the knowledge at your
command, the skills you have mastered,
and
the diagnostic tools you have designed
and assembled,
collaborate with your client
to identify performance gaps in
individual performance, process performance,
and organizational performance
according to your common understanding.

6.16 The Performance System Diagram

Description

This graphic represents the current thinking about performance as an organizational system. It is used by both the International Society for Performance Improvement (ISPI) and the American Society for Training and Development (ASTD).

Explanation

This model comes from Rothwell (1996, p. 7, Figure 2.1). Rothwell credits it to Deterline and Rosenberg (1992). Going back further, its roots can be traced to Tom Gilbert's human performance technology model published first in 1978. It is reprinted here from *ASTD Models for Human Performance Improvement* (1996).

We introduce this model because we are now at its crucial center, defining performance gaps of all sorts, then moving on to analysis of causes for the underlying performance problems represented by those gaps. The graphic is a handy reminder of the many elements of the performance system. Referring to it now can give you reassurance that you've been systematically moving toward positive change and performance improvement.

What You Already Know That Can Help You

Instructional designers and training managers who have grown up with *the ADDIE model* for design of training recognize it as the underlying system of the performance technology model. ADDIE stands for the instructional system design model: Analysis, Design, Development, Implementation, and Evaluation. Trainers who come from an engineering or information systems background also recognize the performance system as analogous to other systems views involving system inputs, throughputs, and outputs. The performance system can be seen to parallel other business systems such as product development, customer acquisition, production, order fulfillment, strategic planning, marketing, engineering, etc.

The Performance System Diagram

Instructions: Refer to this model as you progress through various stages of performance consulting.

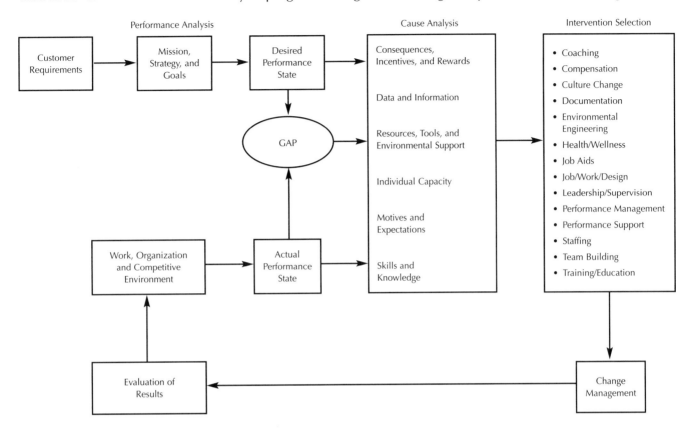

6.17 What Should Be versus What Is Narrative Chart

Description

This simple chart gives you a format for recording each performance gap you find.

Explanation

It is probably worth your time to express the performance gaps that you discover in narrative terms. That is, write down in phrases or sentences what you have found. Keep a notebook of these forms, and organize it around business goals or the company's mission statement.

This fishbone chart is built on the usual places to look for causes of performance gaps, and is based on the work of Thomas Gilbert. Your narrative page could be coded or referenced to one or more of these boxes. Design a reporting form according to your own situation.

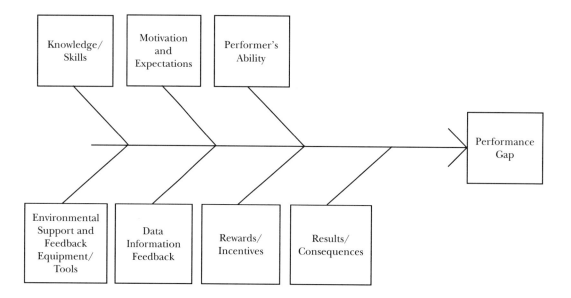

Source: Reprinted from page 14 of *ASTD Models for Human Performance Improvement* by William J. Rothwell. Copyright 1996 by the American Society for Training and Development. Reprinted with permission for this one-time usage. All rights reserved.

What You Already Know That Can Help You

This process of determining what should be versus what is, or defining the performance gaps, is similar to *training needs assessment*, in which a training need is specified. Like the training need, which must be verified, the performance gap needs to be discussed with various stakeholders and verified. Sometimes a narrative exercise can help to clarify definitions for yourself and especially for others.

What Should Be versus What Is Narrative Chart

Instructions: Use this as a worksheet on which to state in narrative terms the "outer limits" of a problem, that is, make a statement about what should the situation be and what the situation is. Then in careful, quantitative terms, if possible, define the nature of the gap between what should be and what is, as you have just stated. The definition and description of the performance gap are needed before you can suggest improvement efforts. Assemble a pile of these worksheets and put them into a binder, organized according to business goals. Code each gap according to the source of its cause(s).

WHAT SHOULD BE	WHAT IS

Source code _____

The Gap
(time, dollars, competencies, quantity, errors, headcount, schedule, etc.)

_____

_____

_____

_____

_____

_____

_____

_____

_____

_____

6.18 "Five Levels of Why" Zero In on Causes

Description

This diagnostic questioning technique helps to find the causes of performance problems.

Explanation

This is an old technique, used frequently in counseling and in facilitating groups. Its objective is to continuously focus your thinking at more and more specific levels to get at the roots or foundations of problems. Adapted by the quality movement, it appears in benchmarking and in problem-solving literature. It's easy to remember and even easier to use. One of its advantages is that, in addition to getting down to root causes, this technique highlights other subproblems along the way. Seeing them in relation to the whole question is often a first step in being able to solve them too.

What You Already Know That Can Help You

Trainers who have experience as *facilitators,* rather than as instructors, relate to this Five Levels of Whys technique. It is a probing technique, similar to that used by a facilitator in getting a person to respond to ever-deepening open questioning. A variant of the Five Levels of Whys is the Five Levels of Whats, which can also be useful to clarify and specify.

"Five Levels of Why" Zero In on Causes

Instructions: After you've identified a problem—a mismatch between where you would like to be and where you are—use this Five Levels of Why technique to further define the performance gap(s) and get to the root cause(s) of the problem. Begin by stating the problem at the top of the chart. Then ask five whys as you go deeper into the causes of the problem. Answer each why question; then probe further against that answer with another why, and so on until you've asked why five times, that is, at five different levels.

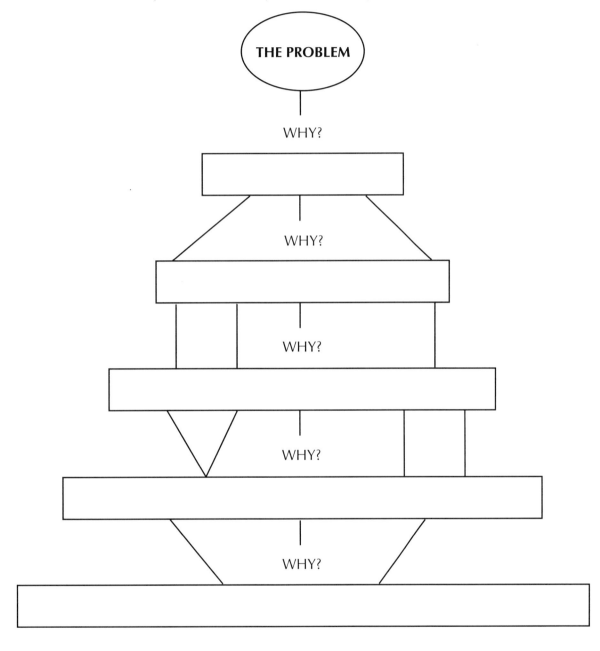

219

6.19 Source of Causes Chart

Description

This documentation form helps to frame the big picture of performance problems in a company. It can lead you forward to solutions.

Explanation

This kind of chart can be used in a small group of employees or other stakeholders, in a focus group, or by a problem-solving team. It can be used by the consultant only as a documentation "spring" before jumping into the solution-finding phase of performance consulting. It is more a documentation form than a diagnosis form. However, the addition of the importance factor makes it useful as a diagnostic tool also. Add as many more sheets as you need; reproduce it on larger paper or turn the paper to a landscape orientation to allow more space for listing causes.

What You Already Know That Can Help You

Trainers on the job today are constantly challenged to evaluate training's effects, particularly on the individual, but also on process and the organization. Kirkpatrick's *Four Levels of evaluation* are standard fare in training seminars of all sorts. The process represented here requires a similar kind of thinking about levels of influence. In most cases, the source of the cause is also where the most effect is found and the place where intervention strategies will be focused.

Source of Causes Chart

Instructions: This is another kind of representation of causes of performance problems. List the causes you have identified down the side of the chart. Then complete the matrix by checking the source of the cause (individual, process, or organization) and by giving each listed cause an "importance" rating now as well as in the future. Rate each item according to a 5-point scale, where 1 is low in importance and 5 is high. Define "future" as three years from now.

List of Causes	Source			Importance Scale = 1 – 5	
	Individual	Process	Organization	Now	Future
1.					
2.					
3.					
4.					
5.					
6.					
7.					
8.					
9.					
10.					
11.					
12.					

Chapter 7

Designing Performance Solutions

Step 8: Choose interventions.

Step 9: Empower employees to make change.

Step 10: Manage the improvement process.

This final chapter takes you into the solutions phase of performance consulting. Ten tools are included. The chapter begins with pointing out some of the important issues in choosing interventions for gap filling for performance improvement. It continues with the all-important step in consulting of any kind: to empower employees to make change. The most professional choice a consultant can make is to depart from an organization with having provided the members of that organization with the power of knowledge and skills to make their own changes, their own improvements.

The book ends with several reminders about managing the improvement process—things the performance consultant can set in place before departing. The book ends essentially where it began: imploring the new performance consultant to be true to the calling of consulting, to step back and figure out what performance consulting is all about, to be steadfast and unafraid to use your existing talents and experience in dealing with learning and organizational development, and to press forward in collaboration with clients to improve business for its many stakeholders.

Tools in Chapter 7

STEP 8

Step 8: Choose interventions.
From a list of identified
desirable states and
from among the many
possible interventions for
making performance improvements,
choose, evaluate, and recommend
the solution that's most likely to succeed.

7.1 What Should Be: The Big Picture

Description

This chart provides space to list all the identified "what should be's"; it also provides a checklist to indicate what kinds of interventions are required. It gives a big picture of optimal performance as well as what's needed to achieve the optimal goal.

Explanation

Completion of this chart gives you a big picture of what you'll need for the optimal states you've identified to be achieved. Seeing this big picture of requirements helps you decide which "what should be's" are possible and probable. This kind of gross overview can guide you into looking for interventions that truly enable performance improvement. Solutions that have no chance of being implemented do no one any good. Near the end of your consulting assignment, you need this kind of overview/review/big view of your options.

What You Already Know That Can Help You

Many *tools in Chapter 2* can refresh you on what performance is all about: above all, think broadly and include input from many and diverse sources. Think about performance at all levels: individual, process, and organization. Use the tools you've assembled and the knowledge about the consulting process that you've gained to thoughtfully and systematically describe "the big picture" with this simple chart.

What Should Be: The Big Picture

Instructions: Make a list of all the "what should be's"—the optimals, the desired states, the performance levels that represent gaps having been closed. Then for each item listed, check off the Requirements. Check as many columns as are appropriate for each. At the end of this exercise, you'll have a big picture of concentration of requirements throughout the organization. Add as many pages as you need.

	Requirements								
What should be	Funding	Policy change	Procedure change	Organization restructure	Redefinition of work	Training			
1. ____________									
2. ____________									
3. ____________									
4. ____________									
5. ____________									

7.2 Intervention Options: Pros and Cons

Description

This chart provides space to list pros and cons associated with each intervention option.

Explanation

A key part of solution finding, as contrasted to problem finding, is the various activities associated with evaluating alternatives. Some call it testing hypotheses; others call it applying filters to each option to determine feasibility.

In the simplest terms, it's figuring out what you believe to be the pros and cons, or plusses and minuses, about each possible solution. These are some of the things to consider when determining pros or cons: the cost-to-benefit ratio; the technical feasibility (can we do it given our present technical capabilities?), the politics of implementation (what key players will/won't align themselves with it?), how strongly the company wants to implement it, how big the obstacles are to getting it done, what will happen if we don't do it, whether we have or can get personnel to do it, whether getting a partial solution is better than waiting for a full solution, etc.

Use the chart to record in phrases or outline form your assessment of pros and cons associated with each possible solution.

What You Already Know That Can Help You

Ever since Tom Gilbert talked about "engineering worthy human performance" in 1978, instructional technologists particularly have been weighing, measuring, analyzing, and correlating factors in human performance, sometimes veering to the right and staying within an instructional system, and sometimes veering to the left to encompass all of organizational performance.

Gilbert's legacy at both ASTD and ISPI (formerly the National Society for Performance and Instruction, during most of Gilbert's worklife) is evident in the system graphic reproduced as Tool 6.16. The Intervention Selection part of the system is reproduced here to reinforce the notion that relationships are very important and that the *performance system* has many variables.

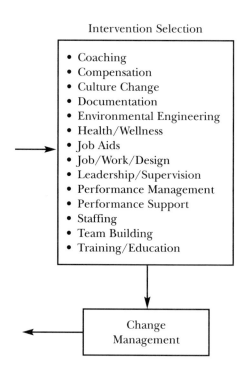

Intervention Selection

- Coaching
- Compensation
- Culture Change
- Documentation
- Environmental Engineering
- Health/Wellness
- Job Aids
- Job/Work/Design
- Leadership/Supervision
- Performance Management
- Performance Support
- Staffing
- Team Building
- Training/Education

Change Management

Intervention Options: Pros and Cons

Instructions: Use this format to record the pros and cons of each option for the intervention you've identified to close a performance gap. By taking the time to list, bullet-style, several pros and cons for each potential solution, you'll more accurately be able to conclude which intervention is the best choice. Add pages as needed.

The gap that needs to be closed _____

Interventions	Pros	Cons

7.3 Solution Evaluation Template

Description

This worksheet helps you structure your thinking about the desirability of a single intervention option.

Explanation

Choosing an intervention means systematically considering variables and ruling out factors that represent obstacles to success. A very useful exercise is to estimate the possibility and probability of success with this intervention, after you have looked at what needs to be done and what needs to be overcome to accomplish your goals. As the performance consultant, you need to go through this kind of analysis for each intervention that you have defined. Do this first by yourself; then verify your point of view with your client. Arrive at a collaborative bottom line.

What You Already Know That Can Help You

As you go through this exercise, remember what you've learned about *problem solving*. Review current literature on the subject, and don't be afraid to apply *creative thinking principles* to the analysis of performance variables in the intervention. Play what-if games with yourself; use analogies and metaphor; put the solution into case studies; extend the expected effects of this intervention into a two-year, three-year, and five-year time frame; break the intervention solution into subsolutions and verify that each part is in fact part of the solution.

Solution Evaluation Template

Instructions: In the spaces, indicate what you recommend in terms of staffing, structure, procedure, timeline, and funding. Add any other categories that fit your circumstances. Then state all obstacles to achieving these recommendations. Give your study of this intervention a possible rating and a probable rating (in terms of 100%). Then fill in the bottom line, that is, your recommended solution. This could be the same as or a modification of the statement of the proposed intervention.

Identified performance gap _____

Intervention proposed _____

<table>
<tr><td rowspan="5" colspan="2"></td><td align="right">**Obstacles**</td></tr>
<tr><td>Staffing</td><td></td></tr>
</table>

		Obstacles
R E C O M M E N D A T I O N S	Staffing	
	Structure	
	Procedure	
	Timeline	
	Funding	

Possibility _____ **of success**

Probability _____ **of success**

The bottom line recommendation regarding this intervention:

_____

_____

_____

7.4 Improvement Proposal

Description

This worksheet suggests elements of a performance improvement proposal, often required in performance-consulting contracts.

Explanation

When you are confident that you have selected the right interventions to solve performance problems, do two things: (1) Write a formal performance-improvement proposal and (2) present it, embellished with graphics and handouts, in a face-to-face meeting with your client(s). Tool 7.4 gives you ideas about what to include in the written proposal. Give your client an opportunity to talk it out with you in person and to seek and receive your clarifications about various elements in the improvement proposal. Have copies of the formal proposal available at the face-to-face meeting, but talk from handouts or overhead transparencies that highlight key elements, that is, fill in the bullet lists with your explanatory dialogue. Leave copies of the formal proposal with the client. Leave your overheads too, if your client would like to use them to talk about the proposal with others in the company. (Remember that this is a collaborative effort.) This important step of choosing interventions is greatly enhanced by client involvement at this stage to verify your choices and to be well-enough informed so that the client can help to disseminate the information that others need for improvement to happen.

The formal performance improvement proposal has four major sections, each of which can be varied slightly to accommodate particular company styles:

1. The performance gap, expressed in terms of cost to the organization.

2. The recommended intervention(s), expressed as benefits to the organization (through processes and individuals).

3. The implementation process, including a timeline and in-process evaluation points.

4. Estimated cost of the recommended intervention(s).

What You Already Know That Can Help You

Instructional designers who've worked in teams are probably familiar with training proposals that result from up-front training analysis. Training managers who have had to develop budgets and justify program expansion also have had to deal with this kind of proposal. Anyone who has had to make a suggestion for *program improvement* based on filling a gap (marketing, engineering, information services, etc.) recognize the same basic proposal structure. It is the basic format for *cost-benefit analysis*.

Improvement Proposal

Instructions: Refer to this worksheet as you write a formal performance improvement proposal to your client. Use this after you have chosen the intervention(s) you intend to recommend. Back up this proposal with files full of related material that justifies your positions in the proposal. State in the proposal that backup material is available on request. Keep the proposal rather short, 5–10 pages at most. Be sure that it is a literate document; check your grammar and usage; be consistent in how you express yourself. Use complete sentences complemented with bullet lists. Include a one-page executive summary if your client likes this extra piece of information. Repeat these four elements of the proposal for each performance gap you have identified.

- **Performance gap.** Describe it in narrative terms. Simply state what should be versus what is for each gap that you have identified. Assign numbers to it so that you can show an estimated *cost* to the organization by continuing this gap. Consider these kinds of numbers:

    Work output numbers, such as items ordered or sold, items manufactured, forms processed, customers served, etc.

    Dollars, including cost per item, cost per project, overtime, cost of absenteeism, cost of accidents, costs resulting from poor forecasting, cost of overhead, cost of payroll, etc.

    Cost of quality, including waste, rejects, rate of error, backorder cost, cost of rework, etc.

    Cost of worklife issues, such as cost of grievances and legal action, cost of employee complaints, cost of turnover, cost of recruitment, etc.

- **Recommended intervention.** Discuss the intervention's effect at organization, process, and individual levels; express these effects as *benefits.* Discuss causes if a discussion clarifies the effects. If several interventions are required for a single performance gap, state the effects and benefits of each.

- **Implementation.** This is easiest done as a timeline with key points highlighted. Include evaluation and feedback points for in-process evaluation, along with the criteria for successful implementation. Be sure that the timeline is inclusive and detailed enough so that the steps of the implementation process are clear.

- **Cost.** Begin this cost section of the proposal with a forecast regarding the *value,* in dollar terms, of the recommended intervention(s). Express value in terms of organization, process, and individual. Talk again in terms of *benefits,* not just cost.

STEP 9

**Step 9: Empower employees
to make change.**
Before you leave an organization,
do your best to facilitate a
change management process
that has employees in
positions of power
to initiate, monitor, and be
responsible for making change.

7.5 Information's Strategic Role

Description

This checklist contains items that refer to many considerations associated with the strategic use of information in an empowered organization.

Explanation

Numerous voices are heard today in the business press pleading for strategic thinking and planning for building corporate knowledge resources through information. An abundance of technological supports for information, a need for a faster and more flexible workforce at all levels, and empowered teams and less bureaucracy all are fueling the heated debate about information's role in high-performance workplaces.

Tool 7.5 highlights some of the issues in this debate. Performance consultants on the cutting edge should incorporate some of these ideas into your proposals for improvement.

What You Already Know That Can Help You

Review recent books on *intellectual capital* and knowledge-creating organizations. Three are recommended: Nonaka and Takeuchi, *The Knowledge-Creating Company*, (1995). Stewart, *Intellectual Capital: The New Wealth of Organizations*, (1997), and Tobin, *The Knowledge Enabled Organization*, (1998). Other books and articles with similar-sounding titles are coming to market frequently.

Companies, too, are making great progress in using information strategically. Several have been prominently featured in training literature and in the general business press: Buckman Laboratories, Andersen Consulting, Ernst & Young, to name a few.

Recurrent themes in these writings seem to be that empowered workers need and want information so that they can use it in practical applications and creatively act on it. Accessibility has to be accompanied by human behavioral standards that encourage experimentation and learning from missteps and mistakes. Performance improvement at all levels—individual, process, and organizational—has a strong relationship to information as a strategic force. Trainers who are readers and thinkers have an edge in developing performance-improvement proposals that take advantage of information as a strategic player.

Information's Strategic Role

Instructions: Refer to this list as you plan your exit from a performance-consulting contract. Incorporate at least some of these ideas into your chosen intervention implementation recommendations.

___ 1. Corporate business information should be shared with all employees.

___ 2. Sharing information requires training in how to use information and why it is important. Training is best done as needed, in context, and by the person who generated the information in the first place.

___ 3. Individuals should be rewarded for how much information they can turn into job knowledge, either by generating information that others can use or by using information that others have generated.

___ 4. Individuals should be responsible for finding, cultivating, and managing their own knowledge resources.

___ 5. The quantity and quality of information dissemination are important.

___ 6. The quantity and quality of information leveraging are also important.

___ 7. Information that is deployed to make customers happy is particularly important to share.

___ 8. Information needs generators, classifiers, and catalogers.

___ 9. Information needs teachers.

___ 10. Technology support for information sharing is critical.

___ 11. Behavioral support for information sharing—how people work together—is also critical. Management's help is very important.

___ 12. Empowerment comes from using information to extricate people from stifling psychological dependence on each other. Personal empowerment through information means freedom to act independently in collaboration with colleagues, with personal accountability for results of one's actions.

7.6 The Importance of Soft Skills: Emotions, Incentives, Recognition, Rewards

Description

This chart contains points pertaining to the soft skills needs of an empowered workforce.

Explanation

Today's flatter, leaner organizations require all employees to develop their emotional capacities to perform their newly structured jobs in companies whose cultures are changing with the times. Employees and employers everywhere need to recognize the importance of the "softer" side of employment. The human relations aspect of facilitating productive work is perhaps more important today than at any time in our recent workplace history. Performance consultants need to plan for the soft skills development of their client's workforce.

A good place to start is with a greater understanding of what Daniel Goleman (1995) calls "emotional intelligence." Empowered employees are leaders of their own work—visionary, in charge, and accountable. Energy, drive, ambition, openness, communicating, negotiating, trusting, being flexible, sharing, seeking—all these are desirable characteristics of high-performing workers in all sorts of jobs. All these have their roots in a well-developed emotional intelligence. Teamwork, remaining employable, developing a sense of self- responsibility, and being a continuous learner all require emotional range and stability.

Part of the classic performance technology model is the role of incentives, recognition, and rewards in fostering better performance. Before departing your performance-consulting assignment, double-check these to be sure that they are aligned with your recommendations for performance improvement. These, too, are best used within a good emotional climate.

What You Already Know That Can Help You

Many management trainers and team trainers have dealt with emotional intelligence subject matter in recent years since the publication of Goleman's landmark book. Prior to this, trainers who were responsible for *diversity training* and training in sexual harassment and affirmative action issues also dealt with emotional issues, although somewhat tangentially.

Today's need for emotional intelligence is driven not by the EEOC, other legislation, or company rules, but by the rapidly changing nature of the structure of companies and the need for employees to be and to act empowered. Performance consultants can help their clients with the action by building emotional skill development into your recommendations.

The Importance of Soft Skills:
Emotions, Incentives, Recognition, Rewards

Instructions: Refer to this chart for ideas to include in your performance improvement proposal. These lists are "tip-of-the-iceberg" points—visible key points—suggesting some of the emotional intelligence requirements in each of these four major areas frequently addressed by performance consultants.

Teamwork

- Choose to initiate action.
- Choose to share knowledge, skills.
- Decide according to group goals.
- Help others with their work.
- Teach someone your job.
- Rejoice in others' successes.
- Accept another's limitations.
- Demonstrate team pride.
- Respect individual differences.
- Coach your teammates.

Continuous Learning

- Participate in dialogue with colleagues.
- Give feedback after systematic observation.
- Accept feedback.
- Learn from mistakes.
- Reserve judgment in favor of exploration.
- Take time for reflection.
- Seek a community of colleagues.
- Figure out how to learn from your job.
- Know your own best learning style.
- Create opportunities for learning.
- Think of work as a learning challenge.
- Recognize when you have learned.

Employability

- Admit deficiencies.
- Chart your own future; stay on course.
- Care about the business.
- Seek advice.
- Accept help.
- Set personal standards.
- Find training that will help you.
- Transfer learning quickly to work.
- Monitor often your employability status.
- Seek recognition for excellence.

Responsibility

- Share your views with others.
- Be articulate and steadfast.
- Do good work.
- Help others to do good work.
- Be accountable for your results.
- Accept constructive criticism.
- Respect parameters and boundaries.
- Be flexible.
- Know how your job furthers the whole.
- Share credit as well as blame.
- Manage stress.
- Leverage your successes.

7.7 Consider EPSS

Description

These guidelines provide help with the decision to recommend electronic performance support systems (EPSS).

Explanation

In recent years, both *Training Magazine* in its fall Industry Survey and ASTD in its annual review of industry best practices have reported on the still small but ever-increasing use of Electronic Performance Support Systems (EPSS) in performance improvement efforts. As employees get more and more used to using desktop computers for all kinds of information gathering and dissemination, mail, commerce, and communication, knowledge assembly, learning explorations, and specific training applications, EPSS applications are not far behind. As a performance consultant, you need to take the pulse of your company to decide whether EPSS might be a good recommendation for performance improvement.

EPSS is envisioned as learning on demand, just enough and just-in-time, available when needed at one's desktop through the touch of a keyboard. A landmark book by EPSS guru, Gloria Gery, (1991) has the subtitle, "How and Why to Re-make the Workplace through the Strategic Application of Technology." This and a quote from Gery herself in *Training Magazine* (February 1998, p. 63) frame the EPSS approach to performance improvement:

> *I've given up on trying to* teach; *now I focus on* support ... *When you support performance, people learn while they're doing. When you support learning—well, who knows what they'll learn? "I learn because I do it; I can't always* do *it because I* learn *it."*

Gloria Gery was inducted into the Training HRD Hall of Fame sponsored by *Training Magazine* and Lakewood Conferences at its recent Conference in Atlanta. She joins other performance technology pioneers Tom Gilbert and Geary Rummler in the HRD Hall of Fame.

What You Already Know That Can Help You

EPSS has often been compared to an *online help* feature—a well-designed help feature and one with great depth, complexity, customization, and sophistication. Like good help features, EPSS applications demand a thorough understanding of the performance required and the help seeker's need and learning capabilities. These systems are not designed and developed quickly or superficially. They require time, resources, updating, maintenance, promotion, and all the other machine–human interface support of any kind that you might have experienced in computer-based training (CBT). Many companies large and small have now had some experience with EPSS; find Gloria Gery in Tolland, Massachusetts. Check web sites and reference information on EPSS available from ASTD, 703/683-8183. Theoretical constructs are found in studies of *situated cognition* and the work of John Seely Brown (1997).

Consider EPSS

Instructions: Refer to these guidelines prior to writing your recommendations for performance improvement. They are especially appropriate for individual performance improvement. Your client might be ready for this ultimate empowerment system. Consider these guidelines; then decide whether your client's performance goals can be achieved through the creation of an EPSS. Or decide to work toward any of these items as part of your performance improvement proposal. More help with any of these items can lead your client into individual empowerment and organizational strength.

___ 1. The definition of performance need is widely accepted throughout the client organization.

___ 2. The client has the capacity for creating and sustaining working relationships and for leveraging talent, knowledge, and skills.

___ 3. The client demonstrates a tendency to see the whole in the parts—to synthesize, not just to analyze.

___ 4. The client has had favorable experience with rigorous task analysis and systematic job design and redesign.

___ 5. The client has a history of focusing on objectives for learning, not objectives for teaching in its training programs.

___ 6. The client has a history of support for learning in context: on-the-job training, coaching, peer to peer training, informal "communities of practice," dialogue in the context of work problems, experimentation, observation, using feedback.

___ 7. Performance evaluation has been regularly done as a developmental support for workers, not as a punitive annual dreaded ritual. Performance evaluation has a positive connotation.

___ 8. The client demonstrates the use of learning aids and cues such as job aids, charts, illustrations, demonstrations, practice sessions, branching to many information sources, simulations.

___ 9. The client has in residence, or the will to hire, software and hardware experts who can design navigation, presentation, and monitoring systems to facilitate the creation of content in context, with performance support as their goal.

STEP 10

Step 10: Manage
the improvement process.

As you leave your client organization,
remember that how performance
improvement is managed is the
client's responsibility.
Your consultant responsibility is
to help your client see the value of
performance improvement strategies
and to lead your client toward
the kinds of management
behavioral changes that lead
to improved performance.

7.8 Build Measurement into the Design of Improvement

Description

This chart lists the output characteristics of organizations, teams, and individuals engaged in improving their performance. These lists are a kind of statement of typical "what should be's" at these three levels—evidence that change can occur. Use them to create specific measures around each, measures such as amount, degree, percent, frequency, perceived accuracy, value, assigned weight/importance.

Explanation

By the time you get ready to write your proposal for performance improvement you and the client both have a good idea of what an improving or an improved company looks like. This chart in Tool 7.8 contains items that describe improved performance, that is, the observable output characteristics, at organization, team, and individual levels. Measures can be assigned to each item, such as the ones suggested at the beginning of the chart. These measures can then be plugged into a measurement system with a timeline and named responsible evaluators, as part of your improvement proposal.

You will often want to depart the company before the changes are implemented. Managing change is the job of company management employees. Consultants can stay on in a facilitative role only under very limited and specific contract parameters. Your job as performance consultant is to give the company the tools it needs to do its work better; your job is not to do the work for them.

What You Already Know That Can Help You

Trainers who develop their own tests based on the learning content of courses know some of the ways to tie objectives for learners to measures for finding out whether those objectives were met during training. This process of building measurement into the design of performance improvement is akin to *test development process in instructional design*. The big difference is that in performance improvement, the scope is much wider, encompassing many more variables.

Build Measurement into the Design of Improvement

Instructions: Help your client build measurement into improvement efforts at various levels. Add other items to each category as fits your situation. Add designs for measurement to your improvement proposal. Give your client the tool of measurement as you prepare to depart the organization.

Periodically ask of items like the ones in these charts: How many? To what extent? What percent? How often? How accurate? At what cost? How important?

ORGANIZATION LEVEL

- A clear and convincing need for change has been made throughout the organization.
- Executive support is demonstrated through the commitment of time, personnel, money.
- Workers know what's expected of them.
- Managers and supervisors know what's expected of them.
- Communication is planned, channeled, networked, focused on improvement.
- Removal of obstacles is planned and implemented.
- Tracking and feedback systems are in place and working.

TEAM LEVEL

The team:

- Is clear about its mission.
- Focuses on results.
- Has a stable internal structure.
- Are clear yet flexible about roles and responsibilities.
- Members support each other.
- Makes decisions.
- Manages conflict.
- Seeks and uses feedback.

INDIVIDUAL LEVEL

The individual:

- Makes improvements in work.
- Improves customer service/customer satisfaction.
- Improves the ratio of personal output to input (productivity).
- Improves profit or margin.
- Reduces waste/improves efficiency.
- Increases skill capacity.
- Contributes to the corporate knowledge system.

7.9 Guidelines for Performance Monitoring

Description

These guidelines suggest key elements in the systematic in-process evaluation of performance improvement efforts known as *performance monitoring*. They provide management with help for institutionalizing performance improvement.

Explanation

An important function of management is to make things happen through facilitation, support, fostering relationships, creating structures, sustaining efforts, maintaining systems, and paying attention to processes. Monitoring performance is one of those processes. It is an essential process because it continuously requires management's involvement in the improvement efforts. The old bit of working wisdom (out of the quality movement) says, "What gets measured gets done."

A distinction is generally made between end-of-process (*summative*) and in-process (*formative*) evaluation. Monitoring fits the in-process model, also called formative evaluation, because its goal is to help to *form* the remainder of the work that a monitoring event documents. Feedback to the performance system is an important outcome of performance monitoring. Making the system work—or changing it—is one of management's key responsibilities.

Don't be afraid to experiment with formative evaluation designs, as you experiment with new work groups and new work ideas. Consider the evaluation of journals, work portfolios, structured dialogue and reflection, case study, scenario construction, etc. Talk to linguists and anthropologists, not just to statisticians and accountants.

What You Already Know That Can Help You

Contract trainers and vendors, as well as trainers who function as internal training consultants, are familiar with *project specifications* and *project status reports*. Performance monitoring is like these in the sense that the ongoing effects of performance improvement need to be periodically and systematically documented, just like the ongoing effects of project work must be documented.

Two excellent sources for monitoring, assessment, and evaluation are:

1) *Assessment Tools and Simulations 1998*, an annotated catalog from the Center for Creative Leadership, Greensboro, NC. 910/288-7210, and

2) *Resource Guide: Evaluation* (1994), a literature review by the staff of ASTD's Information Center, Alexandria, VA. 703/683-8183.

Guidelines for Performance Monitoring

Instructions: Encourage your client management to systematically plan for in-process evaluation of performance improvement efforts at all target levels addressed by your consulting assignment with them. Suggest that this be part of the performance improvement proposal, and write in at least the outline of the performance monitoring plan as the final part of your proposal. The following guidelines are a beginning.

GENERAL GUIDELINES FOR IN-PROCESS EVALUATION

1. Be sure that people know what is expected of them in terms of performance criteria and objectives, and in terms of their responsibilities during monitoring.

2. Adopt a "problems are your friends" attitude; fix what you find is broken.

3. Be reliable and fair. Monitor in the same way, with the same frequency for all objects of monitoring. Publish the monitoring schedule and notify participants.

4. Build quality in. Use findings and feedback to make adjustments.

5. Develop a realistic monitoring schedule and stick to it.

6. Share monitoring information widely. Ask for help and suggestions from all stakeholders.

GUIDELINES FOR CREATING A MONITORING PROFILE (NONQUANTITATIVE)

The easiest way to monitor many performance improvement efforts is to develop a performance checklist using criteria and objectives previously stated, and attach a "qualitative" scale to each item to be monitored. At each successive monitoring session, use a new scale to record your assessment, represented by a point on the line. Draw a vertical line connecting all points on the range line indicating your judgment on each monitoring date. Compare all assessments. For example:

Criterion A	No	Yes
Item 1		
Item 2		
Item 3		
Criterion B		
Item 1		
Item 2		

GUIDELINES FOR SUBMITTING A STATUS REPORT

Some performance improvement efforts can be seen as projects, with beginnings and ends. Monitoring of this sort of effort can be done by completing a weekly one- or two-page status report indicating a list of "accomplishments" and a list of "to be accomplished during the next week" items. Include a space for "commendations and concerns." Keep a folder of all status reports, compare them, give feedback, and make adjustments.

7.10 Remember the System

Description

The model is the ASTD Human Performance Improvement Process Model. It is a graphic representation of all the material elaborated in Section 2.

Explanation

The ASTD Human Performance Improvement Process Model was adapted by William Rothwell from a variety of sources including today's most active and respected performance consultants and academics. These are: Warner Burke, Geary Rummler, the ASTD Expert Advisory Panel, the ASTD Board of Directors, the ASTD Council of Governors, the International Society for Performance Improvement model (Tool 6.16), William Bramer, Joe Harless, Jim Robinson, Dana Gaines Robinson, Richard Swanson, Robert Mager, Marc Rosenberg, and Paul Elliott (Rothwell reference on the following page).

This model comes out of systems theory and is the one in use by practitioners throughout the performance community. It represents an evolution, not a revolution, in how we think about organizational, process, and individual performance improvement. The model allows for wide flexibility within each of its parts, holding great promise for incorporating new ideas in how people learn and work together and why people want to work together. These new ideas are shaping business goals and our experience of competitiveness in ever more connected and relational workplaces.

What You Already Know That Can Help You

The model below is the classic *Instructional Systems Design (ISD)* model, followed for decades by trainers, especially by instructional designers and evaluation specialists. The important thing about this model for trainers is the system—that is, good training has always been seen to be systematic and relational, never as an isolated or self-contained process or product.

Trainers who know and love ISD feel very much at home with the Human Performance Improvement Process Model.

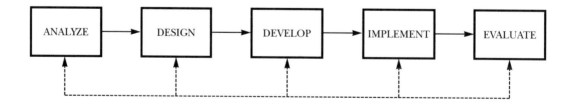

Remember the System

Instructions: Refer to this model and share it widely with your client(s) as you engage in performance improvement together. In this systems view of the process, note that each "box" represents a whole set of challenges with particular disciplines and strategies for success. Learn to see each set of challenges as both separate and in relationship to the whole performance improvement system illustrated by the model.

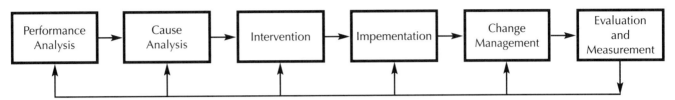

Source: Reprinted from William J. Rothwell, *ASTD Models for Human Performance Improvement,* p. 13. Copyright 1996 by the American Society for Training and Development. Reprinted with permission for this one-time usage. All rights reserved.

Bibliography

American Society for Quality (ASQ). Milwaukee, WI. 414/272-8575.

American Society for Training and Development (ASTD). Alexandria, VA. Information Center, 703/683-8183.

American Society for Training and Development (ASTD). Alexandria, VA. *Infoline*, 800/628-2783.

American Society for Training and Development, *Resource Guide: Evaluation*. Alexandria, VA: ASTD, 1994.

Argyris, Chris. *Knowledge for Action: A Guide to Overcoming Barriers to Organizational Change*. San Francisco: Jossey-Bass, 1993.

Bader, Gloria E., Audrey E. Bloom, and Richard Y. Chang. *Measuring Team Performance*. Irvine, CA: Richard Chang Associates, Inc., 1996.

Bassi, Laurie J. and Mark E. Van Buren. "Sustaining High Performance in Bad Times." In *Training & Development*. June 1997.

Bassi, Laurie J. and Pat Galagan. *Managing Knowledge Assets*, Session M119 at the International Conference and Exposition of the American Society for Training and Development held in Washington, DC. May 1997.

Blake, Robert and Jane Mouton. *The Managerial Grid*. Houston: Gulf Publishing Company, 1964.

Blanchard, Ken, John P. Carlos, and Alan Randolph. *Empowerment Takes More Than a Minute*. San Francisco: Berrett-Koehler, 1996.

Block, Peter. *Flawless Consulting: A Guide to Getting Your Expertise Used*. San Diego: Pfeiffer, 1981.

Bloom, Benjamin S. *Taxonomy of Educational Objectives: Book 1 Cognitive Domain*. New York: Longman, 1956.

Branford, J. and B. S. Stein. *The IDEAL Problem Solver*. New York: W.H. Freeman, 1984.

Brown, John Seely. *Seeing Differently.* Boston: Harvard Business School Publishing, A Harvard Business Review Book, the President and Fellows of Harvard College, 1997.

Center for Creative Leadership. *Assessment Tools and Simulations 1998* (catalog). Greensboro, NC: Center for Creative Leadership, 1998.

Conway, William E. *Waste Chasers.* Nashua, NH: Conway Quality, Inc., 1998.

Deming, W. Edwards. *Out of the Crisis.* Cambridge, MA: Massachusetts Institute of Technology (MIT) Center for Advanced Engineering Study, 1982.

Deterline, W. A. and Marc J. Rosenberg. *Workplace Productivity: Performance Technology Success Stories.* Washington, DC: the International Society for Performance Improvement (ISPI), 1992.

Dewey, John. *How We Think.* Lexington, MA: D.C. Heath and Company, 1933/1960.

Edwards, Mark R. and Ann J. Ewen. *360 Degree Feedback.* New York: Amacom, 1996.

Gagne, Robert M. and Leslie J. Briggs. *Principles of Instructional Design,* 2nd edition. New York: Holt, Rinehart & Winston, 1979.

Gagne, Robert M. and Karen L. Medsker. *The Conditions of Learning: Training Applications.* Fort Worth, TX: Harcourt Brace College Publishers, 1996.

Gardner, Howard. *Frames of Mind: The Theory of Multiple Intelligences.* New York: Basic Books, 1983/1985.

Gery, Gloria. *Electronic Performance Support Systems: How and Why to Remake the Workplace through Strategic Application of Technology.* Cambridge, MA: Ziff Communications Company, 1991.

Gilbert, Thomas. *Human Competence: Engineering Worthy Performance.* New York: McGraw-Hill, 1978.

Goleman, Daniel. *Emotional Intelligence.* New York: Bantam Books, 1995.

Greeno, James. "Process of Understanding in Problem Solving." In N.J. Castellan, Jr., D. B. Pisoni, and G. R. Potts, eds. *Cognitive Theory,* vol. 2. Hillsdale, NJ: Lawrence Erlbaum, 1977.

Guilford, J. P. *Intelligence, Creativity, and Their Educational Implications,* San Diego, CA: Robert R. Knapp, Publisher, 1968.

Hamel, Gary and C. K. Prahalad. *Competing for the Future.* Boston: Harvard Business School Press, 1994.

Hammer, Allen L., ed. *MBTI Applications: A Decade of Research on the Myers-Briggs Type Indicator.* Palo Alto, CA: Consulting Psychologists Press, 1996.

Handy, Charles. *The Age of Unreason.* Boston: Harvard Business School Press, 1989.

Handy, Charles. "A Better Capitalism." In *Across the Board,* April 1998, pp. 16–22.

Harless, Joe H. *An Ounce of Analysis Is Worth a Pound of Objectives.* Newnan, GA: Harless Press, 1980.

International Society for Performance Improvement (ISPI), formerly the National Society for Performance and Instruction (NSPI). Washington, DC. 202/408-7969.

Jonassen, David H. "Instructional Design Models for Well-Structured and Ill-Structured Problem-Solving Learning Outcomes." In *Educational Technology Research and Development,* vol. 45 number 1, 1997.

Jones, Patricia and Larry Kahaner. *Say It and Live It: 50 Corporate Missions Statements That Hit the Mark.* New York: Doubleday/Currency, 1995.

Jones, Sue. *Developing a Learning Culture.* London: McGraw-Hill Book Company, 1996.

Jung, Carl G. *Psychological Types,* 1921; and *The Structure and Dynamics of the Psyche,* 1931. In *The Collected Works of C. J. Jung.* Published in England by Routledge and Kegan Paul Ltd. and in America by The Bollinger Foundation as vol. XX. Translated by R. F. C. Hull. Published also by Princeton University Press, William McGuire, executive editor, Princeton, NJ: 1967.

Kaplan, Robert S. and David P. Norton. *The Balanced Scorecard.* Boston: Harvard Business School Press, 1996.

Kirkpatrick, Donald. *Evaluating Training Programs: The Four Levels.* San Francisco: Berrett-Koehler, 1994.

Kotter, John P. *Leading Change.* Boston: Harvard Business School Press. 1996.

Malcolm Baldrige National Quality Award. *Criteria for Performance Excellence* booklet. Washington, DC: U.S. Department of Commerce, 1998.

Mager, Robert F. and Peter Pipe. *Analyzing Performance Problems: or "You Really Oughta Wanna."* Belmont, CA: Fearon Pitman Publishing, 1970.

Mager, Robert F. *Measuring Instructional Intent.* Belmont, CA: Pitman Learning, Inc., 1973.

Mager, Robert F. *Preparing Instructional Objectives,* 2nd edition. Belmont, CA: Pitman Learning, Inc., 1975.

Maslow, Abraham H. *Motivation and Personality.* New York: Harper & Row, 1987.

Matson, Eric. "Project: You." In *Fast Company.* December: January, 1998.

McLagan, Patricia. *The Models, vol. 3.* In *Models for HRD Practice.* Alexandria, VA: American Society for Training and Development, 1989.

McLellan, Hilary, ed. *Situated Learning Perspectives.* Englewood Cliffs, NJ: Educational Technology Publications, 1996.

Nadler, Leonard and Z. Nadler, ed. *The Handbook of Human Resource Development, 2nd ed.* New York: Wiley, 1990.

National Institute of Standards and Technology, National Quality Program Office, U.S. Department of Commerce, Gaithersburg, MD. 301/975-2036.

Newell, Alan and Herbert A. Simon. *Human Problem Solving.* Englewood Cliffs, NJ: Prentice Hall, 1972.

Newstrom, John and Jon Pierce. *Windows into Organizations*. New York: Amacom, 1990.

Nilson, Carolyn. *Team Games for Trainers*. New York: McGraw-Hill, 1993.

Nilson, Carolyn. *Training & Development Yearbook 1998*. Paramus, NJ: Prentice Hall, 1998.

Nilson, Carolyn. *Training Program Workbook & Kit*. Englewood Cliffs, NJ: Prentice Hall, 1989.

Nonaka, Ikujior and Hirotaka Takeuchi. *The Knowledge-Creating Company*. New York: Oxford University Press, 1995.

Norman, Donald A. *Things That Make Us Smart*. Reading, MA: Addison-Wesley, 1993.

Osborn, Alex. Partner in BBD&O advertising agency, New York, NY, 1954.

Phillips, Jack J. *Return on Investment in Training and Performance Improvement Programs*. Houston, TX: Gulf Publishing Co., 1997

Patterson, James G. *Benchmarking Basics*. Menlo Park, CA: Crisp Publications, 1996.

Quinones, Miguel A. and Addie Ehrenstein, eds. *Training for a Rapidly Changing Workplace: Applications of Psychological Research*. Washington, DC: American Psychological Association, 1997.

Robinson, Dana Gaines and James C. Robinson. *Performance Consulting*. San Francisco: Berrett Koehler, 1995.

Rossett, Allison. *Training Needs Assessment*. Englewood Cliffs, NJ: Educational Technology Publications, 1990.

Rothwell, William J. *ASTD Models for Human Performance Improvement*. Alexandria, VA: American Society for Training and Development, 1996.

Rothwell, William J. *Beyond Training and Development*. New York: Amacom, 1996.

Rummler, Geary A. and Alan P. Brache. *Improving Performance: How to Manage the White Space on the Organization Chart*. San Francisco, CA: Jossey-Bass, 1990.

Senge, Peter. *The Fifth Discipline: The Art & Practice of the Learning Organization*. New York: Doubleday/Currency, 1990.

Senge, Peter, Art Kleiner, Charlotte Roberts, Richard Ross, and Bryan Smith. *The Fifth Discipline Fieldbook*. New York: Doubleday/Currency, 1994.

Smith, Gerald F. *Quality Problem Solving*. Milwaukee, WI: American Society for Quality, 1998.

Stewart, Thomas A. *Intellectual Capital*. New York: Doubleday/Currency, 1997.

Swanson, Richard A. *Analysis for Improving Performance: Tools for Diagnosing Organizations and Documenting Workplace Expertise*. San Francisco: Berrett-Koehler, 1994.

Tobin, Daniel P. *The Knowledge-Enabled Organization*. New York: Amacom, 1998.

Watkins, Karen E. and Victoria J. Marsick. *Sculpting the Learning Organization: Lessons in the Art and Science of Systematic Change*. San Francisco: Jossey-Bass, 1993.

About the Author

Carolyn Nilson, Ed.D., is a veteran trainer with a wide experience base in traditional and state-of-the-art training assignments. Among the corporations and agencies she has served as consultant in training design are American Management Association, AT&T, Chemical Bank, Chevron, Dun & Bradstreet, Lockheed-Martin/Martin Marietta, Nabisco, National Westminster Bank, Bell Atlantic/New Jersey Bell, New Jersey Department of Labor, U.S. Department of Education Office of Vocational and Adult Education, and The World Bank.

Dr. Nilson was a member of the technical staff at AT&T Bell Laboratories Systems Training Center where she developed, implemented, and promoted quality standards in course design and delivery throughout AT&T. She also taught the Bell Labs' train-the-trainer course.

She held the position of Manager of Simulation Training at Asea Brown Boveri/Combustion Engineering, where she managed the training operation and created high-level computer-based training for an international base of clients in various fields of the chemical process industry.

Dr. Nilson was Director of Training for a systems consulting firm with a broad-based *Fortune* 500 clientele in the New York City metropolitan area. In this position, she supervised a staff of training consultants and was responsible for training analysis, design, development, implementation, and evaluation across a range of corporations.

She has been a faculty member for Padgett-Thompson seminars, the Ziff Institute, the Center for the Study of Work Teams, and the U.S. Armed Services Institute. She has been a speaker at national conferences of the American Society for Training and Development (ASTD), and the American Management Association (AMA), and at the Northeast Regional Conference of the International Society for Performance Improvement (ISPI). She received her doctorate from Rutgers University with a specialty in measurement and evaluation in vocational and technical education. Her work has been featured in *Training Magazine, Training & Development, Successful Meetings, Entrepreneur,* and *Fortune.*

Dr. Nilson is the author of fifteen books on training. Among them are *Training Program Workbook and Kit* (Prentice Hall, 1989), *Training for Non-Trainers* (Amacom, 1990), *How to Start a Training Program in Your Growing Business* (Amacom, 1992), *Team Games for Trainers* (McGraw-Hill, 1993), *Games That Drive Change* (McGraw-Hill, 1995), *Training & Development Yearbook 1996–97* (Prentice Hall, 1996), *Training & Development Yearbook 1997* (Prentice Hall, 1997), *Training & Development Yearbook 1998* (Prentice Hall, 1998), *How to Manage Training,* 2nd ed. (Amacom, 1998), and *More Team Games for Trainers* (McGraw-Hill, 1998).

Index